TIPIS
& YURTS

Authentic Designs for Circular Shelters

BLUE EVENING STAR

Lark Books
Asheville, North Carolina, USA

To Gabriel and Niann,
who carry the mandate of the Bright and Morning Star

Published in 1995 by Lark Books
50 College Street
Asheville, North Carolina, U.S.A., 28801

© 1995 by Blue Evening Star

Editor: Leslie Dierks
Art Director: Dana Irwin
Photography: Michael Powers
Illustrations: Kay Holmes Stafford
Production: Elaine Thompson, Dana Irwin

ISBN 0-937274-88-7

Library of Congress Cataloging in Publication Data
Star, Blue Evening, 1956-
    Tipis & yurts : authentic designs for circular shelters / Blue Evening Star.
       p.   cm.
    Includes bibliographical references and index.
    ISBN 0-937274-88-7
    1. Yurts--Design and construction.   2. Indians of North America--
Dwellings.   I. Title.
TH4870.S73   1995
690'.81--dc20   95-6219
       CIP

10 9 8 7 6 5 4 3 2 1

Printed in Hong Kong.

An Apsaroke woman carrying firewood in the winter

C O N T

E N T S

INTRODUCTION

I choose to live in circular spaces because they bring me peace and serenity. The clean edges of the circle heal me, and the wild beauty outside my door inspires me. For 15 years I have lived in tipis and yurts; it's a choice that has challenged and enriched my life tremendously.

My life in these dwellings began as a nontraditional response to the challenge of creating shelter for myself. I cast myself out into the world at a young age and needed a place to get in out of the rain. Unwilling to take a more conventional route, I found my imagination stirred by the idea of living in a world of circles.

Over the years, the process of building tipis and yurts, living in them, and teaching others about them has brought me great satisfaction. I've enjoyed seeing the beauty of a tipi or yurt at night, glowing with warmth and vitality from the wood fire inside, and I've been enriched by the natural sense of community that develops among those who live in circular shelters.

In my studies, I've found that many of the practices needed for coming into balance in a healthy global community can be found in the lives of the peoples who originated tipis and yurts. Tribal peoples in North America and Asia lived in harmony with their environment and valued the quality of life for generations to come over the wealth of a few. Their dwellings are almost magical structures: they are totally portable, unquestionably beautiful, and so simple that they could almost have been designed by Nature herself.

Through trial and error they developed structures that are extremely efficient shelters, even by today's standards. Many principles used in modern homes have their origins in these primitive dwellings. Reflection of the sun during summer, absorption of available heat in winter, blocking the force of the wind, and providing ventilation for fresh air and cooling have been—and continue to be—important challenges for home builders. Many innovative solutions to these problems are exemplified in the simple engineering of tipis and yurts.

Compared to today's standard housing, tipis and yurts are extremely economical and easy to build—and you don't need to be a sheepherder to appreciate their portability. With just a few basic tools and some readily available materials, anyone can build either structure. And when you've finished the construction, there's nothing that matches the joy of sitting within the embrace of your own circular shelter.

Anyone who has ever dreamed of living a lifestyle that is intrinsically bound to nature will enjoy this book. Those who have decided to take the next step and make it happen will find it an invaluable guide and inspiration. I invite you to join the circle.

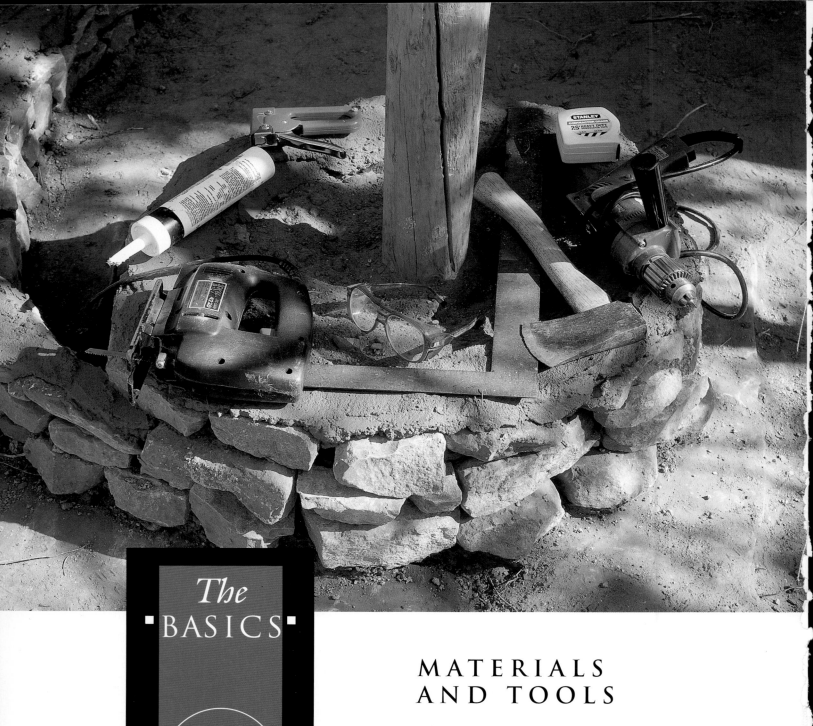

The
·BASICS·

MATERIALS
AND TOOLS

The materials and tools required for making a tipi
vary somewhat from those needed for a yurt, but
both structures have outer coverings that are
made of canvas sewn together into the appropriate shapes. This chapter discusses the recommended materials and tools for making those
outer coverings.

CANVAS

There are various canvas products on the market that can be used for making tipis and yurts. A particularly good choice is sailcloth, which is a cotton canvas that is treated to repel both water and mildew. This type of canvas is well suited for most climates. With proper care it can last 10 years or longer, although it may need a coat of waterproofing material applied after six or seven years.

Synthetic canvas is another good choice and lasts even longer. This material is fire resistant, mildew proof, waterproof, ultraviolet resistant, and rot resistant.

All of the measurements for the tipis and yurts in this book are based upon using cotton canvas, which comes in rolls 3' wide. If you use canvas of a different width—such as synthetic canvas, which is 5' wide—you will have to modify the patterns to accommodate your materials.

THREAD

To sew the canvas by machine, you will need bonded, dacron-coated polyester thread, size 16. Generally this can be purchased wherever you buy the canvas.

NYLON WEBBING

Nylon webbing is a woven fabric that comes in strips of varying widths. Nylon webbing is used on tipis and yurts for making peg loops and ties for holding portions of the canvas in place. Purchase webbing that is either 5/8" or 1" wide.

TOOLS

Sewing the covering for a tipi or yurt requires a minimum of tools. In addition to a work space and sewing machine, you will need these items:

colored chalk, a measuring tape suitable for fabric, a pair of sharp scissors, a razor blade or craft knife, sewing machine oil, large pins, and a ruler.

The best type of needle to use for hand sewing canvas is a glover's needle, which is available at a leather tool and supply store. For your sewing machine, you will need a size 16 or 18 needle. Purchase a few extra to be used when needles break. You also will need extra bobbins for your machine so that you can wind five or six at once and sew for long stretches.

SETTING UP TO SEW

You may be surprised to learn that you don't need a large space for making a tipi or yurt. A minimum 10' x 10' work space is adequate until you get to the step where you need to lay out the whole mass of sewn strips in order to cut the canvas into the appropriate circular shape.

To hold the canvas steady as it is being sewn, it helps to put a large, sturdy table to the left of your sewing machine. If you're sewing outdoors, which can be very enjoyable, spreading tarps or a layer of straw or pine needles on the ground first will help keep the canvas clean.

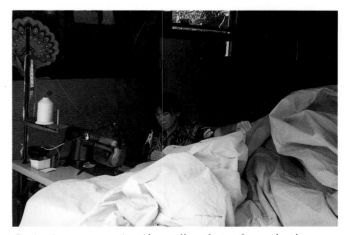

Sewing is more convenient if you allow plenty of room for the canvas to accumulate.

These instructions are primarily designed for those who are sewing on a home-model electric sewing machine. Treadle machines also work quite well. Of course, a commercial-grade "walking foot" or "needle feed" sewing machine makes the job that much easier. Before you start your project, have the machine cleaned and timed by a qualified repair person if this hasn't been done recently.

If you're not using a commercial machine, you will have to make some tension adjustments to accommodate the canvas. To set the machine, you will have to tighten the upper tension and may need to adjust the bobbin tension as well. Tighten the bobbin tension by applying a tiny screwdriver to the small screw on the bobbin. Every slight turn on the screw makes a significant difference. If you don't feel comfortable adjusting the machine yourself, take it along with a piece of your canvas to the repair shop so that they can set the tension correctly.

Experiment with different settings until you get a good stitch. A good stitch is one that looks even: it interlocks not on the top nor on the underside, but within the canvas, where the coming together of the threads is unseen. When sewing your practice stitches, use a doubled piece of canvas.

If you're sewing on a home machine, it may be necessary to take frequent breaks to allow the motor to cool down. Monitor the motor and let it rest if you notice that it appears to be getting hot. Home machines aren't designed for work of this type; however, I have successfully sewn many tipis on a standard home machine, albeit at a slower pace than when using a commercial machine.

Some home sewing machines are such precision instruments that you must tighten the upper ten-

sion every time you increase the number of canvas layers. Other machines (usually the older and simpler models) plow through layer changes easily without requiring tension adjustments. In the event you find that you do need to tighten the tension in order to sew through more than two layers, you probably will need to loosen the tension when you return to the standard two-layer sewing that is most common when making a tipi or yurt.

Always use the exact same thread in the bobbin as you have in the needle. Since the canvas thread (dacron-coated polyester size 16) comes in large spools designed for commercial machines, you may need to wind it onto bobbins to use for the upper thread that feeds through the needle of the machine. Alternatively, you may be able to set up a method of securing the large spool and feeding the thread directly from it into the machine.

Backstitch at the beginning and end of every line of sewing to protect against future unraveling. It is also recommended that you get in the habit of tying off and snipping threads as you go so that you don't have to do them all later.

Some people have no machine or prefer to sew by hand. A tipi or yurt can be sewn very well with a leather awl or with a canvas needle that is threaded with the waxed twine or simulated sinew. By hand it is a long job; by machine, you can expect an 18' tipi or yurt to take from 40 to 50 hours to make.

Enjoy the process of making your own shelter. To avoid fatigue, get up and stretch every hour or so. There may be times when you are tired and things keep going wrong. If so, then take a break and begin again when you are fresh.

SITE SELECTION

CHOOSING A SITE

Making your own tipi or yurt is not an insignificant effort, and the amount of enjoyment it brings is at least partly due to where you decide to install it. It pays to take some time to evaluate a prospective site carefully and to prepare it well before assembling your shelter there.

Your first consideration when choosing a site is the drainage properties of the area. Picture how the rain will flow over the ground, and don't put your shelter in a wash. A site that is higher than its surrounding area is best.

In addition, consider the locations of trees that will shade your shelter at various times of the day and year, and determine the effects on wind caused by trees, shrubs, and nearby land formations. If your site is located on the northeast side of a large tree or clump of trees, your shelter will be shaded for much of the day. Alternatively, you may want to pick a site that takes full advantage of the sun for drying the canvas cover between rains. (If you do place your shelter in the full sun, it will stay cooler if you remove the liner and roll up the sides to catch a breeze.)

ACCESS TO WATER

The nomadic or seminomadic lifestyle made possible by having a tipi or yurt carries with it the responsibility for providing your own water. This can be an enlightening experience because it makes you aware of every drop used.

If you remain close to a settled area, it may be possible to run a hose to your site, where it can be positioned wherever needed and fitted with a spigot. A less convenient but more common approach is to haul water. This can be done in a number of ways, from carrying it by hand in relatively small containers to hauling barrels full of water in a car or truck.

If you enjoy the sunshine, choose an open site for your shelter.

There are many ways to pump water, and you may wish to investigate some of them if you plan to site your lodge near a stream or lake. Many pumps require the use of small motors, but some innovative methods utilize the flow of the water itself to activate the pump.

ELECTRICITY

If your site is in a remote location, there is little likelihood that you might tie into a local power grid. This may be advantageous, for candlelight can be very soothing and romantic. If you need more light for reading, kerosene or white-gas lanterns are useful.

Another alternative is to use 12-volt lights powered by batteries. Twelve-volt appliances are available at RV or motor home supply stores,

and the batteries can be recharged in your vehicle while driving. If changing the battery in your car on a frequent basis is inconvenient, you can use a battery charger. You will need to use an electric outlet or a gas-powered generator to run the battery charger, however.

To generate your own power, you can find gasoline-powered generators with various levels of output. There are also endless possibilities for using photovoltaic (solar-powered) systems. You can research and assemble your own or purchase complete systems that are suited to your needs.

If your primary need for electricity is to provide light, you can minimize the amount required by choosing efficient light sources. One interesting approach is to use halogen lights in combination with mirrors. You can experiment with various positions of the mirrors to send the light into different areas of the lodge.

PREPARING THE SITE

Once you've chosen a site with the best combination of sun, shade, and shelter from the wind, then you must provide a flat area for your tipi or yurt. This generally means flattening the ground itself unless you intend to build a deck that can accommodate an uneven terrain.

The amount of space needed is a circle equal in diameter to your shelter, plus enough room for walking completely around it. Both structures use stakes (or boat hardware, on a deck) to hold them to the ground, so you must provide enough space for these to be installed. If you're building a tipi, provide additional flat space around the front of the tipi for moving the poles for the smoke flaps.

Standing water is a problem for both tipis and yurts. Make the ground flat, but not completely

A wooded location is cool and restful in the heat of the summer.

level. You will have fewer problems with water if your site has a slight slope.

If your shelter is not raised off the ground on some sort of deck, then you will need to provide a trench around it so that rainwater will not seep in around the bottom edges. Dig a trench several inches deep and equally wide, according to the needs of your area. Provide an opening for the water to exit the channel away from the shelter.

FLOORS

The floor of your shelter can be as simple or as elaborate as you desire. Pea gravel is inexpensive and works beautifully. It's comfortable to the feet and holds a fairly even temperature in a moderate climate. If you cover the gravel with straw and rugs, the result is a warm, dry floor. Plywood and rugs over flat ground is simple and quite functional. Other options include rammed earth, adobe, pine needles, or cedar boughs for flooring. Your choice of flooring depends upon how much time, money, and effort you want to expend, how long you plan to stay, and what types of weather you expect to experience.

A basic deck can be constructed from wooden pallets and plywood, or you may choose to build a deck from scratch. Two excellent sources of information on building decks are Ken Kern's *The Owner-Built Home* and *Domebook II* by Pacific Domes (see page 124).

The TIPI

Two Crow Indians riding by a snow-covered tipi

COURTESY WESTERN HISTORY COLLECTIONS, UNIVERSITY OF
OKLAHOMA LIBRARY

Inside the tipi
early morn
Cozy, happy, healthy and warm.
Coming outside is like being reborn
Inside like the womb
Nothing is torn.

KATHLEEN BLUE CORN, 1975

Echo's Call, *photographed by Roland Reed*

HISTORY AND TRADITIONS

No one knows the exact origin of the tipi. Some Indian tribes believe it was an accidental discovery made by a man while playing with a cottonwood leaf. He twisted the leaf into the shape of a cone, then used the cone as the pattern for a dwelling.

Although the tipi is most often associated with the Plains tribes of North America, evidence suggests that it may have an earlier origin. Many subarctic people used tipis covered with bark or the skins of sea animals, suggesting that the tipi was already in existence during the prehistoric migrations of people from Asia to North America.

The ancestors of the Great Plains tribes arrived on the North American continent by crossing a land bridge from Asia across the Bering Straight. The land bridge spanned the 50-mile gap at intervals throughout history whenever the ocean waters receded. The migrants, both animals and people, made the crossing and moved south. Many generations of mankind were involved in these migrations, and the descendants of some of the earliest migrants established their campsites at least 20,000 years ago on the American Plains.

The Great Plains area extends all the way from southern Canada to Texas and westward from the Mississippi River to the Rocky Mountains. Before modern times, it was an open, rolling grassland, broken only by a few scattered hills. There were vast herds of buffalo as well as plenty of other game—mountain sheep, deer, elk, antelope, grizzly bear, beaver, and many kinds of waterfowl. The Missouri River and its hundreds of tributary streams furnished an abundance of water.

The people who lived in the western Plains developed a nomadic existence, following the buffalo herds. They needed a shelter that could be erected and taken down quickly, since their food source was constantly on the move. In place of the permanent earth lodges common to those who dwelled in the river valleys, the Plains people perfected a more portable shelter—the tipi, a Dakota word meaning home.

The tipi meets the needs of a nomadic people with grace and practicality. Its simple yet elegant design makes it superior to other tent structures. Due to its single entrance and smoke hole at the top, the tipi has automatic, controlled ventilation. This ability to ventilate smoke and hot air in the summer plus keep the occupants warm and cozy in the winter makes the tipi a remarkably comfortable structure. In addition, the conical shape of the tipi resists the grip of the high winds that hammer the Plains, and it allows the water to run off during heavy rains.

In the old days, tipis were made from tanned buffalo skins that were sewn together with sinew thread. Before the arrival of the horse, all of the hunting for buffalo was done on foot. It was difficult and dangerous work; the animals had to be stampeded over a cliff or into a trap, such as a stockade or a swamp.

Throughout the greater part of their history, tipis have typically been quite small—just 8 to 14 feet in diameter. This was due not only to the difficulties of hunting buffalo without the benefit of horses or guns, but also to the challenge of transporting a camp by means of dogs and people.

Before the advent of horses, tipis and other essentials were transported on simple sledges

Sioux Camp, *a painting by Karl Bodmer (1809-1893)*

called travois, which were pulled by dogs. Two tipi poles were lashed around a dog, and the load was secured to a platform or netting at the other end of the poles. A strong dog could drag a load ranging from 50 to 75 pounds. Two travois were required to carry a large tipi, which would have been made in two sections for this purpose.

The long tapered branches used to support tipis are called lodge poles, and these were traditionally gathered in the surrounding mountains. Spring and fall are the best times to gather poles because the flowing sap makes the branches much easier to peel. It is important to peel the poles and polish them to a smooth finish so that rain water will stream down the entire length without catching on any snags. Trees typically used then and now for lodge poles include the lodgepole pine, tamarack, aspen, cedar, and fir. Again, until the arrival of the horse, tipi dwellers were limited in how many poles they could carry.

Between 1650 and 1750, the horse was introduced into the lives of the Plains Indians. Horses were first obtained by the southern tribes from the Spanish settlements in New Mexico, and it took nearly a century for the horse to work its way northward to the tribes in Montana and North Dakota.

Once the Plains Indians acquired horses, their nomadic lifestyle took on greater possibilities. They were able to move camp two or three times farther in one day, which allowed them to roam over a much wider territory. More importantly, no longer were they limited to strays or weaker members of the buffalo herds; now they could pursue and kill the choicest animals. They also could accumulate more property and move it farther and faster. A horse could carry 200 pounds on its back and 300 on a pole travois.

The peoples' lives were transformed rapidly and greatly, and like a flood they spread over the

Women of the Blackfeet tribe erecting tipis

Plains. The Plains culture then blossomed, reaching its apex within mere decades. Unfortunately, its decline was equally swift. By 1890 the last of the Great Plains tribes had been erased or broken.

During the period of prosperity and cultural flowering, a tipi required from 10 to 40 hides, depending upon how large the lodge was supposed to be. The average size was about 16 feet in diameter and required about 14 hides. Except for the play structures of the children and the great council or medicine lodges, tipis were seldom made smaller than 10 feet or larger than 25 feet in diameter.

Tipis were made from soft, well-tanned buffalo hides. Women in the tribes tanned the hides for a variety of uses, but for tipis the hides required a number of curing processes to make flexible, water-resistant skins that remained soft even after repeatedly becoming wet. (Untanned skins made unbreakable yet lightweight rawhide that was used for storage containers and drums.)

Tipi covers were replaced every one to three years, but could last for decades if necessary. The favorite season for this task was early summer, since that was the time of year when the hides were most available. Buffalo hides that were gathered in the spring produced the best tipis because the buffalo had just shed their winter hair and the skins were relatively thin.

The women were responsible for making and taking care of the tipis, and little girls began to prepare for this role at an early age. They would play "house" by making their own authentic camps with miniature tipis. Each year the girls would make slightly larger tipis so that by the time they were ready to set up their own lodges and raise their own families they had progressed naturally to the appropriate size tipis.

A Crow Indian camp

23

The women gathered together to make the tipis, which had to be sewn together after the hides were skillfully cut. The sewing was a job made much lighter by the fact that all of the women worked together, much like a quilting or sewing bee.

After a tipi was completed, it was raised up, and the smoke flaps were closed. Inside, a smudge fire was built with partially decomposed, damp wood chips placed on a bed of hot coals. The heavy smoke from the fire began a process of making the tipi water resistant. After one side was thoroughly smoked, the lodge was turned inside out and the process repeated.

From time to time, tipis were turned inside out so that the skins could be cured further by the smoke of the hearth fires burning inside. New tipis were shining white, but after experiencing the curing process and the on-going hearth fires, they gradually blackened around the top. After long use, tipis became almost transparent, and accounts of early travelers often described the beauty of the glowing lodges at night.

The tipi was the perfect home for the people of the Plains, who honored the circle as the signature of the Great Spirit. They found the circle everywhere in nature—the sun and the moon, the cycle of the four seasons, and the circuit of a life—and saw it as a key to understanding their Creator. The circular tipi represented the connection between man and creation, with the poles making the link between earth and sky.

The people who lived in North America for thousands of years before the arrival of the Europeans did so in a sustainable relationship with their environment. According to Grandmother Twylah Nitsch, a well-known, loved, and respected Seneca woman and Elder, this relationship reflected the true meaning of the name Indian. She believes it to be a myth that Christopher Columbus chose this name because he thought he had reached the Indies. Instead, she would like people to understand that the name actually came from the term *los gentes in Dios*, which means "the people of God."

The tribes, without exception, traditionally called themselves by names that translated to mean "the people."

Into the Wilderness, *by Roland Reed, shows a small party traveling with horses and travois through mountainous terrain.*

A Crow Indian camp

According to legend, there was a man who brought back the design for the tipi after he had encountered and slain certain undesirable characters. He saw that Old Man, the Sun, and was told that he had been selected because he was a good man and he was a good warrior. His name was Yellow Leggings. Yellow Leggings had a pet, a bear. When he came back from that Old Man, he informed the people that the spirit of the bear should remain and guard one side of the door poles. He also told them that on his way back he had run across seven brothers who had decided to turn themselves into something that was permanent. In deciding, they said that even things like rocks crumble, but if they were to reside in the sky as the seven stars in the Big Dipper, they would remain forever. So they left this world to reside in the Big Dipper. Now the youngest brother told his brother-in-law, Yellow Leggings, that he would leave behind on earth the spirit of his pet, the mountain lion, to guard the other side of the tipi, and so he tied it to the other door pole. Both the bear and the mountain lion guard the tipi at night. Facing east, the lion is on your left and the bear on your right. The bear is regarded as a fearsome animal; the evil forces stay away because of their fear of it. The mountain lion is also regarded as a fearsome beast.

Henry Old Coyote

Excerpted from *Respect for Life*, edited by Sylvester M. Morey and Olivia L. Gilliam, © The Myrin Institute, New York, 1974.

Sioux Village, Lake Calhoun, near Fort Snelling, *a painting by George Catlin*

An Arapaho camp

Assiniboin boy on horse in front of a painted tipi

In the old days they used to weight the tipi down with rocks. When the Indian moved, he took only his tipi with him and left the rocks. That's why you can find a lot of tipi rings out in the Plains. Once there was an Indian boy who was thrown off this cliff; he hung on to a juniper tree until some Big Horn sheep came along and rescued him. The sheep brought him back to safety and more or less adopted him; they gave him certain powers, and the various animals in the area began contributing to this boy…. He learned something that was to affect the way the tipi was set up. The Badger told him that any time he sank his claws into the ground, nothing could budge him. So the boy came up with the idea of tent pegs. From that boy's time on, the Indians switched from using rocks to tent pegs, because the boy had learned from the badger that if you stick something fast in the ground, you can't move it.

Henry Old Coyote

Excerpted from *Respect for Life*, edited by Sylvester M. Morey and Olivia L. Gilliam, © The Myrin Institute, New York, 1974.

SEWING
THE TIPI COVER

MATERIALS

The major components of a tipi — the outer covering, liner, and door — are constructed from canvas. (Appropriate types of canvas and sewing thread are described in the chapter on materials and tools.) Short strips of nylon webbing provide reinforcement at key locations, and longer pieces are used for peg loops to anchor the tipi and for ties that attach the liner to the frame. The amounts of canvas and nylon webbing required for each size tipi are listed in the table on page 32.

In addition to these materials, you will need special thread for sewing the buttonholes by hand. Either simulated sinew or twine coated with beeswax is recommended. Of the two, simulated sinew is easier to handle. Both can be found in craft and hobby stores.

Also required is wood bracing for the tipi door. For this you will need three branches, sturdy dowels, or 1 x 2 boards, each about 3' long.

TIPI COVER MATERIALS

	Tipi Diameter				
	14'	18'	20'	24'	30'
Strip 1	30'6"	38'6"	42'6"	50'6"	61'6"
Strip 2	30'	38'	42'	50'	61'
Strip 3	28'6"	36'6"	40'6"	48'6"	56'
Strip 4	26'	34'4"	38'	46'	52'
Strip 5	21'	30'10"	36'	43'	46'
Strip 6	*	24'4"	32'	41'	39'
Strip 7		*	26'	35'	35'
Strip 8			*	29'	28'
Strip 9				26'	25'
Strip 10					18'
Total Outer Cover	46 yds.	68 yds.	86 yds.	123 yds.	141 yds.
Length Cut Out from Strip 1	9'	11'	11'6"	15'	15'
Liner Panels	7	10	12	17	20'
Total Liner	24 yds.	34 yds.	37 yds.	50 yds.	60 yds.
Peg Loops (approx. no.)	12	15	17	20	24'
Nylon Webbing	9 yds.	10 yds.	11 yds.	15 yds.	18 yds.

* Use rectangles cut from strip 1.

TOOLS

The tools required for marking and sewing your canvas are discussed in the first chapter, beginning on page 8. Additional tools required include a glover's needle for sewing the buttonholes by hand, a T-square or other straightedge tool with a right angle, and a rope that is a few feet longer than the diameter of your tipi. Make sure that the rope will not stretch when pulled.

CUTTING THE CANVAS

To make a cone-shaped tipi cover from a flat piece of canvas, you must start with fabric cut into the shape of a semicircle. The easiest way to make a semicircular piece of canvas large enough for a tipi is to sew several lengths of fabric together along the selvage edges and cut the assembled piece into the proper shape (Fig. 1).

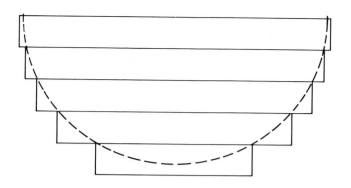

Figure 1

The detailed work takes place on the first length of fabric, called strip 1 for convenience. It is on strip 1 that you will be making the smoke flaps, the reinforced triangle for tying the tipi to the lifting pole, and the buttonholes for the lacing pins and door.

Measure and cut strip 1 according to the length indicated in the table for the size tipi you are making. With colored chalk, mark this (and every other strip you cut) with its identifying number on at least one side of each corner.

Spread out strip 1 on a flat surface. Then mark a rectangle on each end of strip 1 as shown in Fig. 2. Every tipi has rectangular cutouts that are 2' wide, but the length of the rectangles varies according to tipi size. The appropriate length for each size tipi is given in the table.

The rectangles are cut out in order to create the smoke flaps. The canvas that remains in the center, between the cutout areas, will become the smoke flaps.

After cutting out the rectangles, check the table to see if your tipi size calls for a thin strip to be sewn on the bottom. If this thin strip is required, set aside the two rectangles to be sewn together later.

Along the length where each rectangle was cut out, measure 4" down and mark intermittently with chalk. You will be sewing a 4" flap down to form a reinforced edge, which is where the buttonholes will be placed (Fig. 3). Make a 4" straight cut on the inside end of each rectangle; then fold over the canvas along the chalk marks. Make a hem by folding under the raw canvas edge, pin it neatly, and sew it in place.

BUTTONHOLES

Buttonholes sewn by hand are made for lacing up the front of the tipi. This method is preferable to that of installing metal grommets because the grommets eventually rot the canvas underneath and around them.

It is important to match the buttonholes from one side to the other so that the tipi will lace up evenly. To make sure the holes are aligned correctly, lay the two folded-over edges side by side on a table.

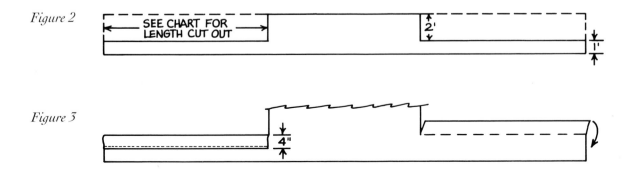

Figure 2

SEE CHART FOR
LENGTH CUT OUT
2'
1'

Figure 3

4"

It's a pleasure to sew buttonholes outside, in the shade of a tree.

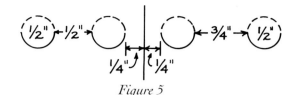

Figure 5

Because there is no need to make buttonholes where the door will be, the first step is to mark the door opening. After making sure that both ends of strip 1 match up (you may have to cut an inch off one side or the other to adjust any difference in length), measure up 12" from the bottom of each strip and make a chalk mark. Then measure another 47" and make another mark. You will want buttonholes just above and just below these marks with 3" to spare (Fig. 4). The 47" gap is where the door opening will be cut later.

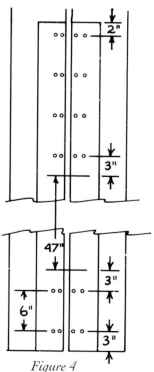

Figure 4

The buttonholes are 1/2"-diameter circles, and there are two buttonholes on either side. As shown in Fig. 5, the set on the right-hand side is slightly farther apart horizontally than the set on the left. This will prove handy when you lace up the tipi through the two sets of holes. The right side overlaps the left, and the closer spacing of the holes in the back makes it easier to slip the lacing pin through both layers.

The sets of buttonholes start 2" from the top and are spaced about 10" apart above the door, ending with the last pair about 3" above the door. To make it easier to mark the holes, I draw the bottom halves of the circles, properly spaced, on a piece of paper. I place the paper where the line of buttonholes should be, then draw the top halves of the circles onto the canvas. After moving the paper, I round out the circles on the canvas.

For stability, two sets of buttonholes should be placed under the door. The two sets are about 6" apart, leaving 3" above and below.

Using a razor blade or craft knife, cut out the buttonholes. It helps to have a small board behind the canvas while the cutting is being done. Another option is to cut out the buttonholes with a pair of sharp scissors by folding each marked circle in half and cutting the visible half-circle.

The buttonhole stitch is used around each hole. To begin, push the needle through the canvas from the back. Loop the thread as shown in Fig. 6 and pass the needle through the loop. Then pull the thread tight. Continue all the way around the hole, taking a stitch

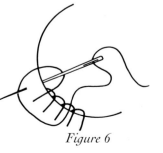

Figure 6

and passing the needle back through the loop, then pulling the thread tight. Finish sealing the buttonhole by snipping a 2" tail of thread and tying two or three square knots. After just a few buttonholes you should be an expert.

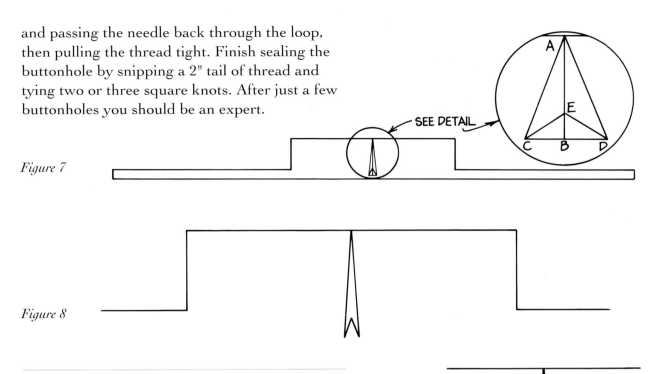

Figure 7

Figure 8

SMOKE FLAPS

The smoke flaps are based on a Sioux design. Begin their construction by laying the middle section of strip 1 neatly on the ground or on a large table. Find the center and mark it with chalk. This point is indicated as A in Fig. 7. Using a T-square or other tool with a perfect right angle, draw a line perpendicular to the edge, from A to B, 32" long. Now mark points 2" to either side of the bottom of the line (C and D in the figure). Using a straightedge, draw a line from A to C and from A to D, thus creating a triangle. Next measure 6" up from B and mark a point, E. Then draw a smaller triangle within the first, as shown in Fig. 7. Finally, cut out the shape indicated in Fig. 8.

Since the small triangle in the center will bear the entire weight of the tipi, you must add canvas reinforcements and webbing ties. Cut two 6' ties from the nylon webbing and pin them to the triangle as shown in Fig. 9. Using two rows of stitching, sew the ties to the edges of the triangle.

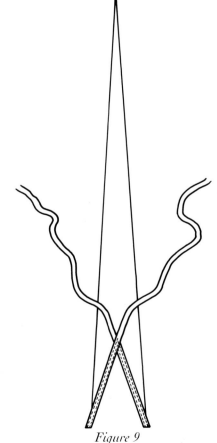

Figure 9

The next step is to add the reinforcement piece. Cut a rectangle approximately 8" x 10" from scrap canvas. Then alter the top of the rectangle to fit the contours of the little triangle as shown in Fig. 10. Pin and sew the reinforcement patch in place. You may sew this reinforcement either onto the front or the back of the tipi, depending upon whether you want to look at it or not. (The side that was folded over and sewn down to form a 4" panel, then marked and sewn to create the buttonholes will become the front of the tipi.)

Nylon webbing is used around the edges of the reinforcement piece to secure it. Pass one end of a length of nylon webbing through a match flame to seal it. This avoids the need to hem the end later.

Now, beginning at the point marked X in Fig. 11, fold the nylon webbing over the edge of the triangle, then along the inside edge of the smoke flap. Without cutting the webbing, open it out flat again and pin it all the way around the canvas reinforcement piece. When you reach the edge of the smoke flap on the left, fold the webbing over the edge of the canvas, matching the effect on the right side. After cutting the end of the webbing, pass it through a flame. Sew the webbing into place with two lines of stitching, one on each edge of the webbing.

You will need pockets on the corners of the smoke flaps for the smoke-flap poles. These must be sewn on the front of the tipi (the side facing

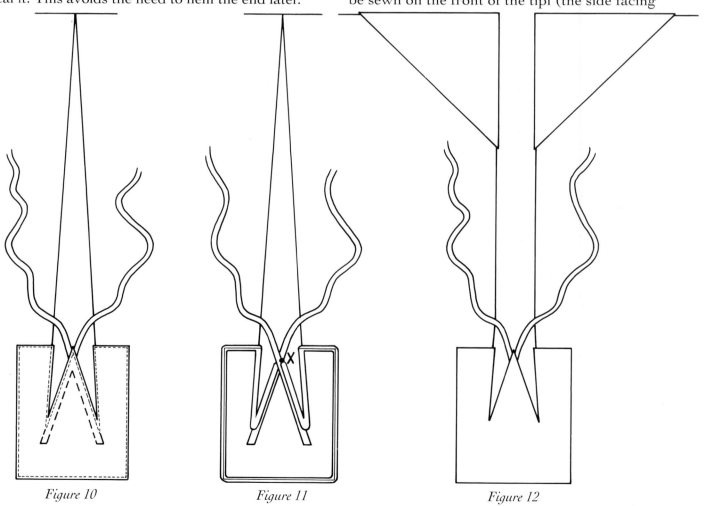

Figure 10   Figure 11   Figure 12

out), which is the side where the flap for the but-tonholes was turned under. Measure and cut two triangles that fit into the indicated corners of the flaps (Fig. 12). These triangles are approximately 10" along each edge. Hem the bottom (open) edge of both triangles by folding over the raw edge and sewing it in place.

To reinforce the smoke-flap pockets and protect them from abrasion by the poles, you need to add small triangular patches on the inside surfaces of the pockets. Cut four triangles about 3" or 4" on each side (Fig. 13). Sew two of the patches, unhemmed, directly onto the smoke flaps. Then sew the remaining two patches onto the back sides of the pockets. Now sew the rein-

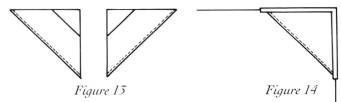

<table>
<tr><td>Figure 13</td><td>Figure 14</td></tr>
</table>

forced pockets into place, remembering to leave the bottoms of the triangles unsewn so that the triangles form pockets. Finally, fold a piece of nylon webbing over the edges of each pocket and sew it in place (Fig. 14). Seal both ends of the webbing by passing them through a flame.

The exposed raw edges running from the pockets to the small triangle between the pockets must be hemmed. Fold the edge over twice and sew it once to create a finished edge. Similarly, hem the raw edges at the bottom end of the smoke flaps, where they meet the top edges of the strips of buttonholes (Fig. 15).

Now sew a piece of nylon webbing (sealed on both ends) onto the top edge of each buttonhole flap, cutting the webbing long enough to extend a few inches onto the edge of the smoke flap (Fig. 15). If not reinforced, the top edges of the buttonhole flaps may wear more quickly than the rest of the tipi.

The final task on the smoke flaps is to cut and sew one buttonhole on each flap, positioned as shown in Fig. 15.

SEWING TOGETHER THE STRIPS

When sewing together the canvas, you want a shingle effect on the outside of the tipi. This is created by sewing the strips so that the water will shed off the tipi and not slip through the seams and into the tipi (onto your head).

The seam you will be using to sew the strips together is an adaptation of the welt seam. This version of the seam takes advantage of the fact that you're sewing together full widths of fabric along their selvages. No further edge finishing is necessary.

Measure and cut each piece of canvas just before adding it to the tipi. If your

Figure 15

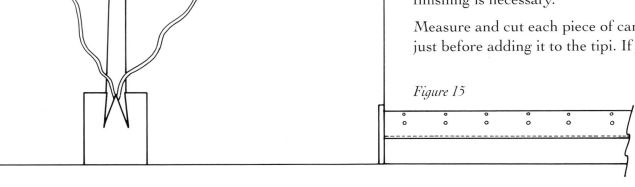

size tipi calls for a thin strip at the bottom, start by sewing together the two reserved rectangles that were cut from strip 1. Using the welt seam described below, sew the two together along one short edge to make a single, long strip (Fig. 16).

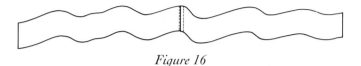

For all tipi sizes, sew the full-width lengths of canvas together sequentially, beginning with the strip that has the highest number (the shortest strip). For example, if the tipi you are making has eight strips, begin by sewing strip 8 and strip 7 together.

Each shorter piece should be centered on the longer one. Mark the midpoint of each strip and align the two marks together (Fig. 17).

Figure 17

For the welt seam, the first line of sewing is done with one strip lying on top of the other, with the edges facing the machine and the bulk of the fabric lying to the left of the needle. Place the strip with the higher number (the shorter one) on top of the other, offsetting it approximately 3/4" from the right edge of the bottom strip. Make your stitching line about 1/8" from the right edge of the top strip (Fig. 18).

As you sew, do not push or pull the canvas; the machine itself does the pulling and you need only to guide the fabric to make a straight line of stitching. At this point, you may want to review the tips given at the beginning of the chapter regarding use of a home machine for sewing canvas.

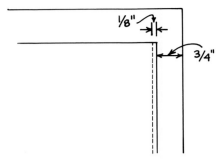

Figure 18

This is where a table set up to your left can be handy, as it will support the weight of the bulk of the canvas while you are sewing. This much material requires that you interrupt your sewing every foot or so to adjust the canvas. Because of the constant need for adjustment, I find it unnecessary to pin the strips before sewing. I simply hold the lengths of fabric together with my hands as I prepare to feed them through the machine. For added security, you may prefer to pin the strips together first.

After you have completed the first line of sewing, pull the bottom (longer) strip out from under the top one and spread it to your right. Fold the shorter strip at the seam so that the longer strip

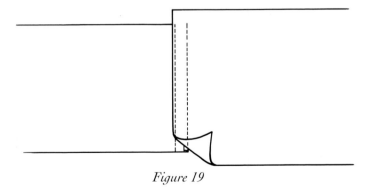

Figure 19

now lies flat on top (Fig. 19). Sew a second seam line about 1/8" from the selvage edge of the longer strip. You will need to fold the longer strip lengthwise so that it can fit between the needle and the main body of the machine.

This procedure is repeated for sewing all of the strips together, giving you a growing mass of canvas on your left. As you cut each new strip from the roll of canvas, label it with the next lower number and position it underneath the preceding strip.

When you get to strip 1, make sure to coordinate the top side of strip 1 with the top side of all the strips you have sewn together so far. (The top of the assembled canvas is the side where the selvages are exposed at the welted seams.) The shingle effect, the position of the smoke flap pockets, and the buttonhole flaps should all match up on the outside of the tipi.

The door opening is large enough to be convenient, yet small enough to offer privacy and protection from the elements.

Even a small tipi requires a large space when you're spreading out the entire canvas.

DOOR OPENING

In the 47" space on strip 1 that is lacking button-holes, draw half of a rounded rectangle on each side. Each rounded half-rectangle is 10" wide at its widest point (Fig. 20). After cutting the door hole, fold under the edges twice and sew them down, forming hemmed edges.

CUTTING OUT THE TIPI

To mark and cut your tipi, you will need rope, chalk, scissors, and two people. You'll also need a clean space large enough for laying out the entire canvas. A residential cul-de-sac, a grassy area in a park, or a school multipurpose room or gym are some likely suggestions. Spread out the tipi neatly, with the top side facing up.

It's best to use rope or twine that is made of cotton or Manila, which doesn't stretch. Nylon rope stretches and won't give accurate results. If you're cutting your tipi outside, it's best to do it on a day with little or no wind.

To mark the tipi, one person should hold one end of the rope at a point on the ground that is cen-tered between the smoke flap pockets and directly above the little triangle. This is point X in Fig. 21.

Holding the rope taut, the second person swings the other end of the rope along the half-circle to determine where to mark your curve. You want to reach under the bottom buttonholes in Strip 1 and clear the corners of all the strips, if possible.

If for some reason you find one or two of your strips coming up a little short, go ahead and mark your curve with the chalk so that the semi-circle comes as close to matching the diagram as possible. (Small scraps can be pieced in later. Just rip out a few inches of the seam on the affected strip and sew the scrap piece in place using the welt seam. See Fig. 22.)

Carefully cut the curve along the chalk line. As you pull away the excess canvas, your graceful tipi becomes visible for the first time. Take a moment to congratulate yourself for a job well done and to appreciate the artistry of tipi making.

Back at the sewing machine, piece in any necessary patches and trim them to match the curve of the bottom of the tipi. The next step is to hem the bottom edge of the tipi by folding over twice and sewing once.

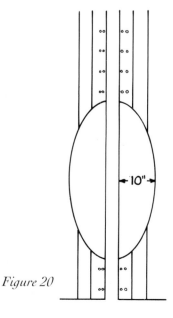

Figure 20

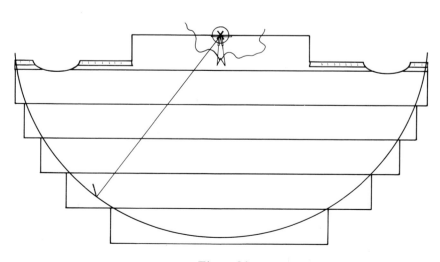

Figure 21

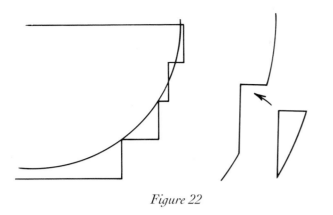

Figure 22

PEG LOOPS

Now refer to the table on page 32 for the number of peg loops needed. In general, peg loops are required at intervals of approximately 4' all along the bottom edge of the tipi. Starting at the door opening, the first and last peg loops are spaced an even distance from the edges of the doorway. The rest of the loops are then evenly spaced around the bottom edge.

Peg loops are made by cutting 4" x 4" squares and 2" x 2" squares. For each peg loop, you will need one square of each size plus one piece of nylon webbing 7" long.

Begin by hemming the edges of all the smaller canvas squares. Now sew one 7" webbing strip to the back of each 2" x 2" square in such a way as to create a loop from the webbing strip (Fig. 23). Now sew one 2" x 2" square (complete with looped webbing strip) onto the front of each 4" x 4" square, sandwiching the ends of the loop between the two squares. Sew each completed peg loop to the bottom edge of the tipi.

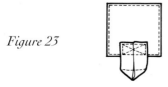

Figure 23

An alternative to these peg loops is simply to gather small, round stones and use them for staking down the tipi. Poke the stones into the canvas to secure them; then attach the stones to the tent stakes with rope. The advantage to this method is that you can vary the positions of the stones and therefore alternate the places along the tipi bottom that are stressed by the peg loops. However, the peg loops described here are very durable and are known to last for the life of the tipi.

THE DOOR

Using scrap canvas, either from the rectangles that were cut from strip 1 or from the canvas left over after cutting out the tipi, sew a rectangle that is approximately 55" x 25". Mark an oval shape within this rectangle with chalk (Fig. 24); then cut the oval for the door.

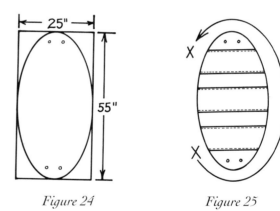

Figure 24   *Figure 25*

Measure and cut three strips of canvas about 9" wide and as long as your door is wide. Turn under the edges and sew the strips onto the door as shown in Fig. 25. The strips serve as pockets for thin pieces of wood that gives the door some stoutness.

Now hem the outer edge of the door by folding under the outside edge twice. Hem only the area of the door that corresponds to the area shown between the two Xs in Fig. 25, leaving one end of each strip open to accommodate a piece of wood.

To brace the door, use 1" x 2" boards, slim but stout tree branches, or dowels. Cut the wood a few inches shorter than the pockets so that you can easily sew the open end closed. After slipping the wood pieces into the pockets, hem the remaining edge of the door so that the entire edge is finished and the pockets are sealed shut.

The final step for the door is to cut and sew buttonholes as indicated in Figs. 24 and 25.

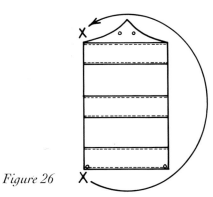

Figure 26

Another option for the tipi door is shown in Fig. 26. This door is 56" long and 32" wide. A buttonhole should be cut and sewn by hand on each corner of the bottom; these are used to stake down the door from the outside when leaving the tipi. The top of the door is an inverted V shape and has two buttonholes near the point of the V. To install the door, the top buttonholes are slipped over one of the lacing pins above the door opening.

LINER

No tipi is complete without its liner. The liner not only helps minimize drafts, but it also prevents dampness inside the tipi. The cushion of air

between the outer covering and the liner provides insulation against cold and wet weather.

The liner of the tipi is created by making several panels and sewing them together. Every size tipi has a specific number of liner panels, and this number, together with the total yardage needed for the liner, is included in the table on page 32.

Liners generally are 6' tall, and these plans assume that you will use canvas that is 3' wide. (Cut two sections from the 3' canvas; then sew them together to make each 6' liner panel.) If you are working with a different width, then you will have to adjust these plans accordingly. If you are using canvas that is 5' wide, you have the option of cutting your panels directly from the canvas roll and making them 5' high instead of the usual 6'. Another approach is to cut 12" sections to add to the 5' panels, making them 6' tall.

Begin measuring panel sections by laying out several feet of canvas from the roll (without cutting) and mark one top section 3'7" on top and 4'6-1/2" on the bottom, as shown in Fig. 27. This will be used as a template to mark the rest of the top sections.

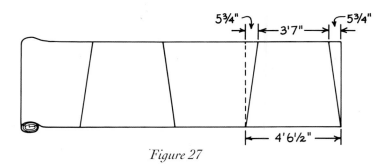

Figure 27

After cutting out the template, turn it so that the wider edge is on top, and lay it on the canvas to mark the next top panel section. Similarly, turn the template for each new panel before marking and cutting it so as not to waste canvas.

Now mark and cut a template for the bottom panel sections. Each bottom section is 4'6-1/2" on top and 5'8" on bottom. Using this template, measure and cut the required number of bottom sections as you did above.

After all the liner sections have been cut, they must be sewn together. Join one top section to one bottom section using the same welt seam used to sew the tipi strips together. The direction of the "shingles" doesn't matter here because the liner will be used inside the tipi. Continue until all of the sections have been joined into panels.

Lengths of nylon webbing are used to tie the liner in place inside the tipi. Each panel has two ties on the top and one on the bottom, except the very first panel, which has an extra tie on the top for stability. Cut three nylon webbing ties, each 10" long, for every panel in your liner. On two-thirds of the ties, seal the ends by passing them through a match or candle flame. Seal the remaining one-third of the ties on one end only.

To complete each panel, sew two webbing strips on the top and one on the bottom. For the top, use strips that have both ends sealed, placing one in the middle and the other at the rightmost edge (Fig. 28). On the very first panel, sew a third

strip on the top at the leftmost edge. For the bottom, place a single strip on the back of the liner, midway across and 8" up from the bottom. The strips used for the bottom ties have only one end sealed. Hem the end of the strip that is attached to the canvas.

Now sew the liner panels together along the cut edges, using a simple double stitch. Lay two panels together, with one on top of the other, and stitch them together about 1/8" from the right edge. Stitch again about 1/8" to the left of the first sewing line (Fig. 29).

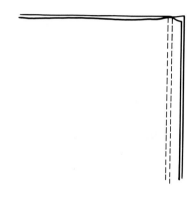

Figure 29

Continue to add one panel at a time, sewing each one to the growing liner. You have the option of sewing all of the liner panels together or of assembling the liner in two or three sections. The advantage to keeping your liner in sections is that the smaller pieces are somewhat easier to install when putting up the tipi. They are also easier to fold and transport, especially when dealing with larger tipis and longer liners. The disadvantage is that when the liner is installed, there will be gaps between sections rather than a complete circle of insulation around the inside of the tipi.

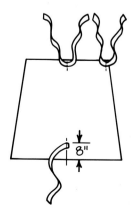

Figure 28

PITCHING A TIPI

ORIENTING YOUR TIPI

Prepare the site and decide what type of flooring you want, as described in the chapter on site selection. Then determine how you want to orient your tipi.

It's traditional to face a tipi toward the east, which allows you to greet the sun when you first emerge from your lodge in the morning. When choosing which direction to face your tipi, be mindful of the prevailing wind direction. If your smoke hole faces directly into the wind, you will have problems when you have an open fire inside the tipi. The wind will drive in the rain and blow the smoke back inside your tipi.

POLES

Getting poles is a major task, but not one that is impossible. Some sources sell tipi poles (see the listing at the back of the book), or you can cut your own.

On the west coast of the United States, both eucalyptus and redwood are available for making tipi poles. Eucalyptus is heavier than redwood and tends to crack, but it has an appealing fragrance. In mountainous areas, there are typically many trees suitable for making poles: varieties of fir, pine, spruce, and cedar. As its name implies, lodgepole pine is the very best.

Bamboo poles are great except for their many ridges, which cause drips during rain. I find bamboo poles especially useful for smaller tipis. Sometimes you can harvest bamboo yourself or find it in a nursery.

If you can locate a burn site, you may be able to cut poles without having to cut green, living trees.

If you don't have access to private land with suitable trees, contact your local Forest Service representatives to inquire about permits for cutting trees that will be suitable for tipi poles.

Your poles should be straight and thin. Ideally the diameter at the bottom should be between 4" and 6", and the diameter near the point where the poles are lashed together should be approximately 1-1/2" to 2".

The poles are lashed together at a height equivalent to the diameter of your tipi plus the distance you choose to have your tipi canvas up off the ground. Generally your tipi canvas should be anywhere from 2" to 9" off the ground. The length of your poles should be at least 2' more than the height of your tipi, but it's preferable to have them 4' or 5' longer. The height of your tipi is the same as its diameter.

Every tipi has two smoke-flap poles plus a total number of tipi poles that is divisible by three. The total number of poles required for each size tipi is shown in the table below. The smoke-flap poles are shorter than the tipi poles and may be somewhat crooked. The smoke-flap poles should be approximately 1' less in height than the height of your tipi. For all practical purposes, you can have fewer poles than the number indicated in the chart; your tipi simply will not be as filled out when pitched.

TIPI AND SMOKE-FLAP POLES					
Tipi Diameter	14'	18'	20'	24'	30'
Total No. of Poles	14	17	20	23	32

After choosing appropriate limbs for your poles, cut and peel them. A chain saw will make the job of cutting the poles and slicing off side branches much easier and faster. If you prefer to do it by hand, use a hatchet or hand saw to cut the poles, and use a hatchet or machete to trim off the branches. A draw knife is the best tool for peeling off the bark.

To remove the bark, place one end of the pole on a sawhorse or rock; then straddle the pole and pull the draw knife toward you. If there are nubs left after slicing off the branches, use a sharp axe to smooth the surface. Pruning saws used for fruit trees also function well in this capacity. Another option is to use a metal wood file to smooth out the poles, but wait until the poles have dried out somewhat before filing them.

Poles are easiest to peel if they are still green, especially when the sap is running in the spring or fall. After peeling, let the poles season for three weeks, if possible. While the poles are seasoning, support them so that they won't warp. Turn the poles every few days because the portions exposed to light and air tend to dry more quickly, which may cause them to warp.

If some of your tipi poles are slightly bent to start with, you can straighten them while they're drying by placing them against a tree or on a tripod and by turning them daily. Another method for dealing with crooked poles is to toss them into water for a week. This is most feasible if you can find a pond or lake in which to contain them.

Once your poles have dried, it's a good idea to sand them with a moderately coarse grade of sandpaper. An electric sander will speed and simplify this task considerably. After sanding, the poles can be preserved using two parts turpentine and one part linseed oil. Finished poles should be so smooth that raindrops will roll right down them without dropping into the tipi.

Some people shape the butt ends of their poles into points. This causes the poles to pierce the ground and hold the tipi steady.

Tying colorful streamers to the top ends of the poles adds real visual delight. The streamers dance and twirl in the wind and stir the hearts of all who have the pleasure of seeing them. They also serve a practical purpose—they perfectly describe the direction the wind is blowing.

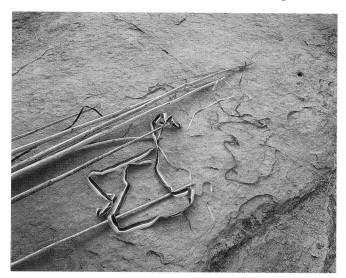

When tied to the tops of the tipi poles, decorative streamers will dance in the wind.

ROPE, LACING PINS, AND STAKES

Rope used for tying the tipi poles together must be of a type that does not stretch. Half-inch-diameter Manila rope is a good choice, as is a thick cotton or good quality nylon rope. Any type of rope, including cotton clothesline, may be used for installing the liner and the smoke flaps.

Chopsticks or dowels work well for lacing pins. For a more rustic effect, use straight tree branches, each about 8" long. Peel the bark and carve one end of each pin for easy insertion into the buttonholes. Another method for lacing up your tipi is to secure the holes with short lengths of rope.

For stakes, ready-made varieties are available wherever you find camping equipment, or you can make your own. Any hardwood is good for making stakes; just cut the branches 10" long and peel away the bark. Sharpen one end to a point and notch the other end for catching the peg loop.

ROPE, PINS, AND STAKES

Tipi Diameter	Length of Rope for Tipi	Liner	Flaps	Approx. No. of Lacing Pins	Approx. No. of Stakes
14'	27'	85'	22'	14	11
18'	36'	120'	24'	18	16
20'	40'	130'	24'	20	17
24'	50'	165'	30'	24	23
30'	75'	200'	40'	30	32

Stack the poles to one side and spread out the tipi canvas.

SETTING UP THE TRIPOD

With all the preparations done, now you're ready to set up your tipi. You'll need five people to set up a lodge that is 18' or larger. At least two people are required for setting up smaller tipis.

Lay the tipi canvas on the ground, with the top side (the side with the flat welt seams) facing down. Because you will be measuring the tripod on the tipi before erecting it, you must place the tipi out of the way of the site where you will be pitching it. Cut the rope for the smoke flaps in half and attach one length to each flap by tying it to the buttonhole at the bottom corner.

The tripod consists of the north pole, the door pole, and the south pole. All of the tripod poles must be strong, tall, and straight.

Lay the door pole over the north and south poles as shown in Fig. 1, placing the door pole one-third the distance around the tipi from the right edge. Make sure the tripod poles cross directly over the base of the little triangle on the tipi canvas.

Each tripod pole extends an equal distance beyond the bottom edge of the canvas. The

Set the tripod poles so that all three overextend the canvas by an equal amount.

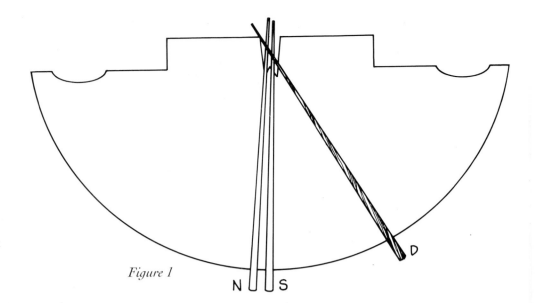

Figure 1

N S

D

amount of overhang determines how high the tipi will sit off the ground. In the summer, you may want to have your tipi well off the ground so that you have plenty of air flowing into it. Six to nine inches is recommended.

If you are in an area where there is a problem with insects, you may want to have the tipi come almost to the ground. You can create air flow during the day by unfastening a few peg loops and rolling up the canvas. In most places the bugs are worst at dawn and dusk, so you can simply roll down the sides at these times.

Another option is to pitch the tipi with the sides several inches off the ground, then place mosquito netting over the open area to protect the inside of the lodge from bugs. Mosquito netting can be obtained from army surplus stores.

If you are going to have an open fire pit in your tipi, then you should pitch it so that a good amount of air will flow under the cover. When the liner is in place, the tipi works as a natural chimney and pulls the smoke out the top through the smoke-flap hole.

After you've erected the tipi a few times, you can mark the points on the tripod poles where they are tied. Then you no longer will need to measure the tripod each time.

Using the 1/2" Manila rope (or equivalent), tie the apex of the tripod together. You may first tie a clove hitch (Fig. 2), then wrap the rope around

Figure 2

three or four times, and finish with a few knots, or you may forego the clove hitch and simply tie the rope around the apex of the tripod three or four times, finishing with a few knots. What's important is that you don't tie the rope in between the poles, but only around them, and that you tie the tripod together very securely.

Tie the tripod together with one end of the rope.

At least two people are required to raise the tripod and push it into position.

Don't cut the rope; leave the long end hanging free for use later.

Now carry the tripod over to the site, being careful to keep the angle of the poles the same, or the rope may loosen. Place the door pole to the right of where you want the door to be. Now position one person on each of the numbered spots, as shown in Fig. 3.

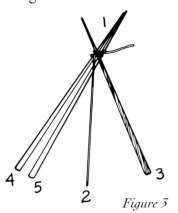

Figure 3

To erect the tripod, follow these steps:

- Person 1 walks forward and pushes up the tripod.
- Person 2 gathers the slack from the rope and supports the weight of the tripod.
- Person 3 prevents the door pole from slipping.
- Person 4 prevents the north pole from slipping.
- As soon as possible, person 5 swings the inside (south) pole around so that the tripod stands up.

Once the tripod is standing securely, check its position by standing in front of the door pole. The north and south poles should be an equal distance from the door pole, and the space between the north and south poles should be less than that between the door pole and the north and south poles.

LAYING IN THE POLES

You now have three spaces between the tripod poles to fill in with tipi poles. Ideally, each space should contain an equal number of poles. Choose one of your poles to be the lifting pole. It must be strong enough to support the weight of the whole tipi cover; however, the pole itself shouldn't be too heavy because you will have to lift the pole and the tipi together.

If you wish to do so, now is the time to tie colorful streamers to the tips of the poles.

After setting aside the two smoke-flap poles and the lifting pole, lay one-third of the remaining poles to the right of the door pole. Place each pole by first putting the butt end in the desired location on the ground, then walking the pole into an upright position. The procedure for large poles is to have one person hold the butt end with his foot or hands while another (or several others, if necessary) walks the pole upward with hands and arms, pushing the pole up and into place. Each pole lies directly on top of the preceding pole in the front crotch of the tripod. You often need to hold these poles in place until you secure them with rope.

Now lay one-third of the poles to the left of the door poles in the same crotch as all the poles already placed. Hold them to keep them from slipping.

Lay the remaining poles (except the lifting pole) in the space between the north and south poles. Leave a space open near the middle for the lifting pole. The configuration of your poles should be similar to that shown in Fig. 4.

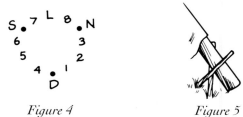

Figure 4   *Figure 5*

When the poles are laid in, they make a star-burst pattern against the sky.

With the poles in place, you must tie up the bundle. Take hold of the rope that is hanging down from the tripod and walk four times around the tipi. Traditionally this is done in a clockwise direction. As you walk, pull the rope tightly around the bundle. After making four circles around, tie the rope to one of the poles. During heavy winds, stake this rope firmly into the ground in the center of the tipi, or tie it to something very heavy that has been placed in the center of the tipi.

The only time my tipi came close to falling down was when I lived for a winter on the east slope of

Walk around the tipi four times, pulling the rope tightly.

the Sierra Nevada Mountains in California. My 18' tipi didn't actually come down, but as the wind came down the mountain in a fury, the shape of the tipi changed dramatically as the poles crept further and further in toward the middle.

The remedy for this is to stake down the poles. It may be sufficient to stake down only the tripod poles, unless the wind is blowing its heart out. Then you must stake down each pole individually and check all of the poles from time to time to make sure they're not coming loose.

To secure each pole, make a cross by pounding two stakes into the ground on the inside of the pole (Fig. 5). Tie a rope around the pole and stakes; then tie the loose end of the rope to a third stake pounded into the ground a few feet away from the pole. This system is the best for heavy winds.

On a calm day, you may avoid staking the poles and proceed directly to installing the canvas cover. Take the lifting pole and lay it on the tipi cover in the exact same position where the north and south poles lay earlier when measuring the tripod. The lifting pole should be touching the inside of the tipi. Take care that the lifting pole extends the same distance over the bottom edge of the tipi as did all three tripod poles. Using the webbing on the small triangle, tie the tipi securely to the lifting pole. Be sure to tie it well! It is

Tie the tipi cover securely to the lifting pole.

helpful, especially when pitching larger tipis, to reinforce this attachment by tying a length of rope over the already tied webbing and triangle.

Fold back the smoke flaps under the tipi so they won't get stuck against the poles as the cover is installed. Then fold the tipi cover in from both sides toward the middle and lash it loosely to the lifting pole. Be sure to tie it low enough on the pole so that it's within reach for loosening after the tipi is up.

Now carry the lifting pole to the tipi poles and place it in the remaining spot between the north

Use the lifting pole to maneuver the tipi canvas into position. Once the pole is in place, open the canvas…

*...wrap it around the poles, and
bring the front edges together.*

and south poles. Again it is easiest, especially with large tipis, to set the butt end of the pole in place first, then raise the pole into position.

Wrap the cover around the poles as you would place a cape around a person's shoulders. If the smoke flap becomes caught, it can be maneuvered free with a pole, or you can pull the tipi canvas to loosen it. Bring the cover together at the front and fasten it by placing the first lacing pin into the top buttonholes. To reach this buttonhole on a large tipi you may need to step on a box, a chair, a person's shoulders, or a ladder.

Friends are welcome to help with the lacing.

Insert the lacing pins to close up the front of the tipi.

Lace up the front of the tipi, putting each lacing pin through four buttonholes. The two buttonholes that are closer together go behind the two buttonholes that are farther apart.

Now go inside the tipi and push out the poles. Position them all equally far apart. Don't move the tripod poles unless you must. If you move one, then you must move all three to maintain the proper triangular shape. The lifting pole also should not be moved.

Any wrinkles in the canvas probably will be smoothed out once the canvas is staked down.

There is frequently a problem with some wrinkles running horizontally and you may finish up with a large sag at the edge of the bottom of the smoke flap. This is caused by setting the tripod too wide and can be adjusted only by starting over again. It makes no practical difference — only an aesthetic one — if you have a few wrinkles. After putting up the lodge a few times, you will learn how to avoid them.

Stake down the tipi canvas all around. Either slip your stakes directly into the peg loops and hammer the pegs into the ground or tie 2' of cotton or nylon rope onto each peg loop. Pound the stake into the ground and tie the rope to the peg; then hammer the peg farther into the ground. On rocky ground, you can tie the peg loop ropes around heavy rocks to secure the tipi. If you have your tipi on a deck, you can mount boat hardware on the deck and tie your peg loop ropes to that.

SMOKE FLAPS

Slip the smoke-flap poles into the small pockets on the smoke flaps. Smoke flaps are adjusted, according to wind and weather, with the poles and with the ropes that are tied to the buttonholes at the bottom corners of both flaps. Tie the ropes to available trees, or stand a pole in the ground in front of the tipi and tie the ropes to it. British tipi dwellers call this a "charlie stick" and report that they usually use a forked stick, with one branch for each cord. An alternative to using trees or a charlie stick is to place a brick or rocks over the rope ends to hold them in place.

You will find that there are many ways to position the smoke flaps. If it's raining, for example, and you wish to let smoke out of your tipi without letting the rain in, you can position the flaps to do this. First drop one flap back so that it's at a 45-degree angle to the smoke hole. You can keep this flap in a taut position by maneuvering the pole and rope accordingly. Then move the other flap into a position directly over the first flap so that the hole is covered completely by the second flap. Set the pole and rope in such a way that an opening is left between the two flaps to allow the smoke to escape.

On other occasions you may wish to close the flaps completely. To do this, drop one flap back entirely and wrap the other flap completely around to cover the smoke hole. The smoke-flap pole must be brought around the front of the tipi and tucked tightly into position to maneuver the flaps into the fully closed position.

INSTALLING THE LINER

Using a little less than half the rope designated for the liner, suspend the rope from pole to pole inside the tipi about 5-1/2' up the poles, winding it around each pole to secure it in place. Then wind the rest of the liner rope from pole to pole about 4" or 5" up from the bottom. The purpose of the liner is to insulate the tipi. Tie the liner onto the upper rope with the ties that run all along the top of the liner. Tie the bottom end of each liner panel to the lower rope. Beginning

with one end of the liner, tie it to one side of the door and work your way around the circumference of the tipi.

When it rains, water droplets tend to collect on the liner rope and fall into the tipi. To avoid this, place two twigs under the rope as it winds around each pole (Fig. 6). Then the raindrops will flow between the twigs and continue down the pole and into your trench. It helps to run your finger down each pole when the rain first begins to make a path for the water to follow.

Figure 6

KEEPING YOUR TIPI DRY

There are four basic methods for protecting your tipi from rain, and you should be able to improvise materials for all four ways.

The first is to use a rain bonnet. This is a square of canvas or heavy-gauge plastic, approximately 10' x 10', placed over the tips of the tipi poles. For this method, you must have poles that are uniformly about 2' taller than your tipi. The bonnet works well in rainstorms, but it's greatly challenged by high winds. To help hold it in place, tie ropes around the edges of the bonnet and attach the ropes to nearby trees, pegs, or heavy rocks. This method allows you to stay dry while still keeping a fire burning in your tipi.

The second method, called a hat, was developed in Britain and is an efficient method for keeping rain out of a tipi. It consists basically of a large square of waterproof canvas that fits over the tops of the poles to keep them dry. The size of the square depends upon the length of the poles extending above the tipi. Make the square a bit larger than the longest pole section above the tipi. In one corner, make a pocket just like the one on each smoke flap. Then sew buttonholes in the remaining three corners.

Slip a tipi pole into the hat's pocket and tie a rope to each of the other three corners. Lift up the pole with the hat dangling from its tip and lay the pole snugly against the back of the tipi. Now pull the two outside ropes around to the sides of the tipi and stake them into the ground in locations for maximum rain protection. The rope in the back is staked down behind the tipi.

The third method is ideal for light rain situations. A piece of plastic or canvas is tied to the poles inside the tipi, just under the bundle. Tie rope to all four edges of your inner bonnet and, using a ladder, secure it to the poles. It's a quickly executed rain catcher that is adequate for a short rainfall. You may need to tip the water out from time to time if the rain is prolonged or heavy. To keep rain from dripping into the tipi, you will need to place twigs between the ropes and the poles as explained previously.

The fourth method is a variation of the third. To the middle of your inner bonnet, connect a hose. The water collects in the bonnet and flows down the hose, behind the liner, and into your rain trench. Use strong plastic mailing tape to secure the tube to the bonnet. For the tape to adhere, the bonnet must be made of plastic. If you're concerned about the attachment of the hose to the plastic bonnet, you can tape a small funnel to the middle of the bonnet and fasten the hose to the funnel.

RAIN SKIRT

A rain skirt is effective when you have extended rainy periods. It's made of canvas and plastic and is designed to go around the bottom of the tipi to keep the lodge dry and to prevent mildew on the bottom edge of the tipi cover.

The plastic is sewn to the canvas, and the canvas has ties that are secured to a rope hung from pole to pole (Fig. 7). The bottom liner rope can

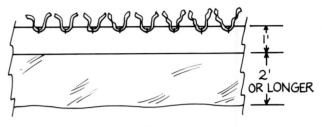

Figure 7

be used for this purpose. Tie the rain skirt to the rope while pushing the rain skirt behind the tipi poles as you go. Push the plastic under the tipi cover and into your trench, arranging it around the peg loops, ropes, and stakes as best you can.

DISASSEMBLING THE TIPI

Disassembly of a smaller tipi requires from two to five people, depending upon the size of the tipi and the experience of the people. If your tipi is very large, you will need quite a few people to handle its weight.

To take down a tipi, simply reverse all of the steps you followed when assembling it. Begin by removing everything inside, except the liner. Then remove the door.

To take down the cover, first pull out all of the stakes from the ground and untie the ropes from the peg loops. Then remove the lacing pins from above the door opening. Roll the two sides of the tipi cover away from the door, toward the back of the tipi. Now wrap the tipi cover around the lifting pole. (This is the only pole that has the tipi cover tied to it at the top.)

To bring the pole and the cover to the ground, one person should place a foot at the bottom of the lifting pole while the others pull the pole straight back and away from the bundle of poles. Using all available hands, work together to lay the pole and its burden on the ground. The person who is holding the bottom of the pole in place with his foot should keep the bottom of the pole from flying up into the air.

If you have a liner installed, now is the easiest time to remove it. Unfasten all of the ties and fold the panels neatly. Then remove the ropes that were suspended from pole to pole to hold the liner.

Now, taking the rope that is hanging down from the top of the tipi, walk around the tipi and unwind the rope from around the bundle of poles. Remove the poles, one by one, in the reverse order in which they were placed. To take down the poles, it's best to have one person holding the bottom of the pole in place while another eases the pole down to the ground.

Now the tripod is all that is left standing. Position one person at the door pole and one at the north pole to keep each one from slipping. If you have a large tripod, have a third person hold the rope that is hanging from the top of the poles. This person should take some of the weight while the tripod is coming down.

To bring down the tripod, lift up the bottom of the south pole and swing it around until it's par-

Unwind the rope from around the poles by walking in the opposite direction around the tipi.

allel to the north pole. Then bring the two remaining sides of the tripod gently to the ground by walking up the poles with your hands. While this is going on, two people should remain at the bottoms of the poles to keep them from flying up from the ground.

Be sure the canvas is dry when you fold it up.

TAKING CARE OF YOUR TIPI

Always tend your fires. It's strongly recommended that you cultivate the practice of never leaving a burning fire, candle, or lantern unattended in your tipi. Keeping a fire extinguisher, shovels, and a supply of water on hand at all times is a wise precaution. If you're in an isolated location, you should establish some means of communicating to others in case of emergency, perhaps with flares or a CB radio.

During storms, a tipi should have people nearby on a regular basis. If there is any leakage, you can place bowls out to catch it. Keep the outer stakes firmly in the ground, and maintain a fire

to dry out the canvas. Living in a tipi allows you to experience the elements even while you are sheltered from them.

You can smudge the tipi by burning sage or cedar in a shell or ceramic bowl. After lighting the dried sage or cedar, blow out the flame and spread the smoke around your lodge. It not only smells sweet, but it also purifies the area.

If your tipi gets any holes in it, you can patch them by gluing canvas patches over the holes with a canvas glue, usually available in awning shops. When your tipi is in storage, be extra careful that it is completely dry and that it will stay dry.

The ·YURT·

A Mongolian yurt silhouetted against the mountains

© Lois R. Wheeler

HISTORY

The yurt of today differs little from that of Genghis Khan's time about 800 years ago, when it was the only means of shelter for the nomadic Mongols. Its design is well suited to the region of its origin, combining extraordinary stability with ease of transport. Its round shape withstands the high winds of the steppes, thus fulfilling the need for a formidable shelter; at the same time, the

Members of an extended family standing next to their yurt

© LOIS R. WHEELER

yurt is collapsible and easily moved, which is an essential feature for a nomadic lifestyle.

In Mongolia this type of dwelling is called a *ger*, which means "felt tent." The word yurt actually means "homeland" or "domain," but the word was mistakenly adopted by Russian, Turkish, and Western writers and is widely used to describe the home itself.

The country that is the homeland of the Mongolian people is a high plateau, most of it over 3000 feet above sea level. The climate, except in the far north, is extremely dry. It is also harsh, with fierce winds and great variations between winter and summer temperatures. The Mongols say that summer is like heaven and winter like hell.

Traditionally a yurt was made with a light,

collapsible wooden frame that was covered with sections of felt. A hole was left uncovered at the center of the top so that the smoke from the yak dung fires could escape. The frame was constructed from willow or any other suitable and available wood. The willow branches were lashed together with the tough desert grass of the Gobi. This desert grass was also made into rope that was wound around the entire structure in order to lash down the sections of felt on the outside.

Felt making is an ancient craft that was invented in central Asia. Unlike most fabrics, felt isn't woven; it's created by rubbing and squeezing moist wool together. The result is a thick but

In the shadows of the mountains, a small herd grazes among the yurts.

© LOIS R. WHEELER

Inside a yurt, a woman sits on her bed.

Ready to move on to the next destination

lightweight material. In the winter, the Mongols covered their yurts with as many as eight layers of felt, which provided good protection against cold, wind, and rain.

Many Mongols relocated their yurts by loading them onto carts that were pulled by yaks or camels. They say nowadays that an average-sized yurt (about 16 feet in diameter) can be pulled by four camels or two jeeps. In the past, the large yurts—spanning as much as 30 feet in diameter—that belonged to the khans were said to have needed from 20 to 40 yaks to move them. Transporting a village of yurts was a rather ponderous expedition, moving along at the pace of the accompanying herds of sheep and ponies that were seeking fresh pastures.

In his book *The Mongols*, E.D. Phillips describes a theory suggesting that the yurt was an adaptation of the tipi: the cone of the tipi was widened and augmented with a wall around the bottom to provide more space and stability. This theory is supported by research into the customs of nomadic peoples throughout the Arctic and sub-Arctic regions. There are many photographs of structures that are hybrids of tipis and yurts, some with tipi poles for the roof frames and others with the more traditional yurt-style frames.

With its smaller, lighter structure, the tipi was well suited to the lifestyle of the hunter, while the roomier but heavier yurt better accommodated the nomads who tended their herds of sheep, horses, yaks, and camels. This is not to imply that the Mongols were merely tame herders of sheep. They were fierce warriors, riding into battle astride their tough little ponies, and they conquered vast portions of Asia.

The horse was probably the single most important element of Mongolian life on the steppes. The Mongols are credited with evolving horse warfare and travel, due mainly to their invention

Left: The entryway to this yurt is decorated with traditional color and design.

Above: A view of the sky hole, inside the yurt

Below: A trio of Mongolian yurts

COURTESY PROFESSOR URGUNGE ONON, UNIVERSITY OF CAMBRIDGE

of the saddle and innovations in shooting from horseback using a short, sinew-strung bow.

These were a people whose lives, when they weren't in battle, were full of tasks. Daily chores included guiding the wagons, making bows, arrows, and saddles, loading pack animals, building carts, caring for the herds, milking, making butter, dressing skins, making garments, and making felt for the yurts and their furnishings.

Inside the yurt, there was also much activity, but the furnishings and goods were arranged in a precise order. The location where one sat was clearly prescribed according to whether one was the master or mistress of the yurt, an honored guest, or a servant.

The yurts contained so much life that they must have appeared to visitors from other cultures to be bursting at the seams. Young children often played near the door, bags of fermenting mares' milk hung around the walls, and young lambs were taken inside on cold nights. Visitors were always treated with the utmost regard and respect, although many early Western visitors made the social blunder of touching the door jamb as they passed through the yurt door, an act that was considered very impolite.

The Mongols had no desire to live in permanent buildings; even though they had amassed great wealth through their conquests, they continued to use yurts as their homes. When the Russian czars attempted to control the nomads of Turkestan, they built small castles for the tribal khans, hoping to induce them to stay put. The khans pitched their yurts nearby and used the buildings as cattle stalls.

No matter what changes modern life has brought to the Mongols, many still prefer to live in their

A single yurt stands among other dwellings in Ulan Bator.

© LOIS R. WHEELER

Mongolia: Building a Yurt

© HOWARD SOCHUREK

A Mongolian yurt motel

© Lois R. Wheeler

THE YURTS

Like silver islands floating in the bright blue sea
The snow-white Mongol yurts stand out from the verdant plain,
The numberless herds and flocks at pasture are like scattered pearls,
They ripple like gentle waves that play at the edge of the sea.

Untouched by the fate that topples dynasties,
Why should the Mongol yurts be victims of the mighty dynasties yet to arise?
The Mongol yurts stand in ranks under the generous light of the sun in the golden firmament.
And still they stand forever under the silver rays of the crescent moon.

An island may be submerged by the power of the surging waves.
Pearls may be swept away in the rush of a torrent.
Like the Onon River the world changes and flows on,
But Mongol yurts in their ribbed and latticed frames
Remain untouched by time or season.

From the fire-flame on the hearth the pale blue smoke eddies upward
Trailing out endlessly to reach the sky.
By ancient tradition we cherish and honor the fire and the hearth,
Rejoicing in our felt covered Mongol yurts.

U. Onon

Excerpted from *My Childhood in Mongolia* by Urgunge Onon (translated by Owen Latimore).

What he did there may have been deceptively simple.
He ate raw garlic and instructed breadmakers
about his likes and dislikes.
He insisted his yurt face south on the blue river.

He told his best friend that the Slavs were collectively
disoriented which meant he and his buddies
would have to invent practically everything.
The Slavs were entirely tentless and, therefore, airless.

He said the Slavs were having a love affair
with singular ideas and the formalization of numbered
events.

The story of the primitive floated over the river in thin blue
light under one full moon after another.
Genghis talked of collecting the light and taking
it home with him, but he knew the imagination could be
pushed only so far.

And that's when the Slavs began to talk to him of reorganizing
his hordes whereupon he ate more and more garlic and talked
endlessly to them of the viability of living in tents.

Shortly thereafter, all kinds of special interest groups came
to see him. Each group had proof.
Each group had a trade and a peculiar history to lay
down in front of him.
None of them wanted to talk about tents.

That's when he went back inside his yurt, closed the flaps
and went to sleep.
He dreamt of the beautiful blue light over Prague
in early morning.
And he dreamt of the flat wide prairies of Mongolia
and the singular shapes of land stretched out over land.

He dreamt that the whole world belonged inside a tent
and that everything outside was extra.
All the rest was secondary.
All the rest would have to be entirely imagined.

When he woke, he laughed a loud booming Mongolian laugh
and the laugh floated up over the water and the yurt
and out into blue light.

He was a man, this Genghis Khan, who insisted on travelling
light, and he dreamt of a universe so deceptively simple
that it couldn't be traced even if it could be imagined.

Wild was Genghis, the dreamer who came and went,
loved yurts, left little, slept long and late, ate garlic,
adored the color of the sky most of all.

Wild was Genghis, travelling man, imagining practically
everything as he travelled the wild world,
his wide dreams unrecorded, quiet,
entirely of hordes and yurts and blue after blue
light, flying out over the Vltava in the 12th century
in the land of the Slavs.

CHARLENE LANGFUR

A painting (artist unknown) of a yurt being assembled

yurts. In the towns and cities many continue to live in yurts, often placing fences around them to approximate the privacy of nomadic life on the steppes. The yurts themselves have changed very little in appearance over time, although many now are prefabricated structures with aluminum frames, wooden doors, and canvas covers.

Through the centuries, the yurt has become a sacred universe to its inhabitants. The yurt itself represents the earth, and the hole in the roof is the sun. The hearth is the heart of creation and is treated with honor. No rubbish is thrown into the fire; instead, offerings are poured into it, mixing with the smoke and rising with the house deities up to God. The hearth is the most sacred area and is referred to as the "square of the earth."

Sign of the times: a motorcycle parked in front of a yurt. Note the stove pipes coming though the roof of the yurt on the right.

DESIGN OVERVIEW

The yurt described here is an adaptation of the traditional Mongolian design, incorporating Western styling and available materials. In this design, the wall lattice, rafters, and hub are constructed from stock lumber, and the outer coverings and windows are made of canvas, plastic sheeting, and mosquito netting.

Other practical changes have been made in the traditional design. The pitch of the roof has been made steeper to improve the yurt's ability to handle heavy rains and snow, and for added comfort, the walls have been made taller.

This design has been developed with an emphasis on portability to make the yurt easy to assemble, take down, and transport. Even the largest yurt can be taken down easily and fit into a small truck.

The frame is made in two parts: below is a vertical wall lattice about 6' high, and above is a domed roof frame made of poles that converge like the spokes of an umbrella around a small, central hub.

The wall frame is built with 1 x 2 lumber bolted together into maneuverable lattice sections called *khanas*. Two or more khanas are bolted together into a circle, forming the yurt wall. This wall also includes a door frame. When unbolted, the individual khana sections compress for easy transport.

After the walls are erected, a steel cable is fastened along the top edge and tightened using a turnbuckle. The cable functions as a tension ring, and it sustains the greatest amount of the roof's weight while distributing the weight evenly throughout the wall lattice.

Rafters, which are notched at one end, are fitted onto the steel cable. The top end of each rafter is drilled to receive a bolt that fastens it to the central hub.

MATERIALS

The lumber used for the yurt frame should be #1 select, kiln-dried, straight-grain wood, with no knots. Douglas fir is best, but other comparable lumber (preferably close grained) is acceptable. Warped pieces are not to be used.

The khanas are made with 1 x 2s, each cut 6' long. The total number required depends upon the diameter of your yurt; see the table below. For the rafters, you'll use 2 x 2s (and 2 x 3s for larger yurts) cut to the length specified in the table. (If you use wood that is softer than Douglas fir, buy 2 x 3s rather than 2 x 2s for all your rafters.) The door frame requires three 2 x 4s, two 6' and one 8' long, and two 2 x 2s, each 5'3" long. The door itself is made with 11 1 x 2s, each 6' long.

Additional materials required for the yurt frame include one sheet of 5/8" exterior plywood, 1/4" x 2" hex bolts with matching nuts and two washers per bolt, and cling-ons (Simpson Strong-Tie H1 brackets or equivalent).

These hardware items are required for the door frame:

- Small box of #6 x 3/4" Phillips flat-head screws
- Approximately 40 2"-long Phillips flat-head screws
- Small box of #6 x 1-1/2" Phillips flat-head screws
- Wood glue
- 2 - 5" internal-angle mending plates (with matching screws)
- 2 - 5" rectangular mending plates
- 5 eyelet screws, in a size large enough to accommodate your rope (see the materials section in the chapter on assembly)

- 12' of hook and loop tape

And these for the door:

- 8 flat-angle mending plates, 4 - 3" and 4 - 5"
- 22 rectangular mending plates, 8 - 4" and 14 - 5"
- 2 door hinges, as thin as possible
- 2 door handles, gate type
- 1 screen door catch
- 2 slide-type door latches (optional)

In addition, you will need two pieces of canvas, each slightly larger than 3' x 5'1" for the door. If you want to have one or more windows in your door, follow the procedure described for installing windows or skylights, starting on page 90.

TOOLS

Minimal equipment is needed for making a yurt. Just two electric tools are required: a jigsaw and an electric drill. For the saw, you'll need blades suitable for cutting plywood and for cutting wood up to 2" thick. Two drill bits—5/16" and 1/4"—and a Phillips screw bit are used.

Required hand tools include a miter box, T-square or corner square, staple gun and staples, crescent wrench, measuring tape, pencil or marking pen, four adjustable clamps, goggles, and gloves.

To hold your work steady, a pair of sawhorses, or equivalent structures, is very handy.

CONSTRUCTING THE KHANAS

Begin by making a template exactly 6' long. This will be used to measure all of the 1 x 2 pieces and must be cut accurately. Trim it with a jigsaw if necessary.

Measure and mark the template for five holes at 16" intervals. As shown in Fig. 1, each hole is marked exactly in the middle of the 1 x 2. Measuring from one end, mark the holes at 4", 20", 36", 52", and 68". Now recheck your measurements to make sure the marks are all 16" apart. Drill the holes straight through, using the 5/16" bit.

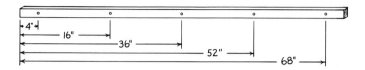

Figure 1

Check every 1 x 2 to make sure it is exactly 6' long. If any require sanding on any surface, do so now. Then use the template to mark a number of 1 x 2s. Marking and drilling are easier if you lay the boards across two sawhorses.

If your skill at drilling allows you to make a straight hole, you can clamp two or three boards

The wood must be drilled carefully so that the khanas line up perfectly when they're assembled.

together for speedier drilling. Mark and drill all of the 1 x 2s *except* the 11 that will be used to construct the door.

	YURT FRAME MATERIALS				
	Yurt Diameter				
	14'	18'	20'	24'	30'
Khanas	2	3	4	5	6
1 x 2s (Khanas)	75	120	130	160	190
Bolts	185	300	325	400	425
Washers	370	600	650	800	850
Nuts	185	300	325	400	425
Cable Length	58'	60'	65'	78'	96'
Hub Diameter	2'	3'	3'	3'6"	4'
Cling-Ons	10	18	20	26	30
2 x 2s (Rafters)	10	18	20	20	21
2 x 3s (Rafters)				6	9
Rafter Length	7'6"	9'4"	10'5"	13'	16'

To assemble the lattice work, first determine the number of 1 x 2s in each khana. Calculate this by dividing the total number of 1 x 2s for your lattice wall by the number of khanas required for your size yurt. For example, if your yurt has three khanas, divide the number of 1 x 2s by three.

Now take half the number of 1 x 2s for one khana and lay them so that they are slanting slightly to the right on the two sawhorses (Fig. 2). Making an X, lay five or so (to begin with) of the remaining half of the 1 x 2 pieces for that khana on top. As you set the top boards onto the bottom ones, line up the holes.

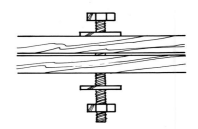

Figure 3

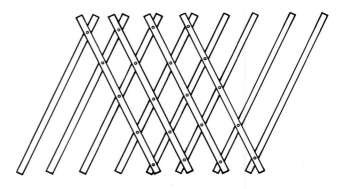

Figure 4

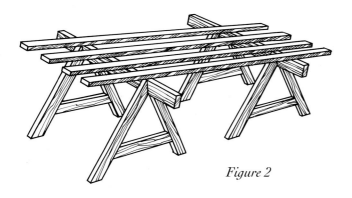

Figure 2

Insert the bolts so that one washer is on each side of the two boards (Fig. 3). The first 1 x 2 to bolt into place is one that lines up with the top of the leftmost 1 x 2 and with the bottom of the fifth 1 x 2 (Fig. 4). Keep adding boards and bolting them in place in the same pattern until all of the 1 x 2s counted out for that khana are connected (even if some of the 1 x 2s are not bolted in every hole). Your first khana is assembled.

Sometimes it isn't easy to get the bolts into the holes. Assuming that your holes are measured correctly and drilled properly, you need only to open up the lattice a bit or close it down by stretching it until the holes line up and the bolt slips in easily. The nuts are tightened by hand.

Now assemble the other khana(s) the same way. *Caution:* each khana must be consistent regarding front and back in order to fit together. Front and back are determined by how the bolts are inserted when constructing the khanas. The head of the bolt is on the front side of the khana (which will be the outside of the yurt), whereas the nut end of the bolt is on the back side of the khana (which will be the inside of the yurt wall).

Once assembled, lean the khanas against a wall and test to see if they are compatible for bolting together. You may need to add or to take away a 1 x 2 to line up the khanas for a perfect fit. Be sure that you have all of the khanas facing the same direction (bolt heads all facing out). Mark a "B" (for bottom) on every fifth or sixth 1 x 2 along the bottom edge of each khana.

If you're planning to transport the khanas in a vehicle, you may want to drop wax on the ends of the bolts or tap them with a hammer so that the nuts don't rattle off. The hammer will damage the threads slightly (use the prong end of the hammer directly on the threads) and keep the nuts from slipping off while you're traveling down the road. Don't tamper with any of the bolts that must be removed and replaced when attaching one khana to another.

RAFTERS

The 2 x 2s (and 2 x 3s for larger yurts) for the rafters all must be cut to the exact length for your size yurt, as noted in the table. Notch each rafter on one end by drilling a hole about 1/2" from the end, right in the middle of the board. Then, using the jigsaw, make two cuts that form a notch in the end of the rafter (Fig. 5).

Figure 5

An option is to drill a small hole through the edge of the rafter near the outside end of the notch (Fig. 6). This hole is useful when the yurt is pitched because you can slip a nail into it to prevent the rafter from slipping off the steel cable during the assembly process. This secondary hole may be drilled before or after making the notch in the rafter.

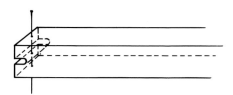

Figure 6

At the opposite end of the rafter, use the 5/16" bit to drill a hole 3/4" from the end. This hole allows each rafter to be fastened at the central hub.

HUB

The diameter of the hub for each size yurt is indicated in the table on page 75. Cut a circle the correct diameter from the plywood, and sand each surface as needed.

For convenience, the brackets that are fastened to the edge of the hub are called *cling-ons*. These are actually Simpson Strong-Tie H1 brackets (or an equivalent product).

The cling-ons must be modified to be used. Clamp each one down to a sturdy table and enlarge the middle hole in each of the two protruding "arms" by drilling through it with the 1/4" drill bit (Fig. 7). Then bend the bracket up about 1/2".

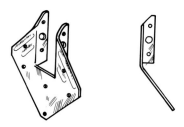

Figure 7

Next mark the placement of each cling-on around the hub's edge. There is one cling-on per rafter, and the cling-ons should be equidistant from one another around the hub.

Using the 3/4" screws, fasten the cling-ons to the hub's edge using the drill and screw bit. Use the four holes in the main body of each cling-on to fasten it to the hub. The cling-ons are fastened to the underside of the hub so that the arms are tilting down.

DOOR FRAME

Cut two lengths, each exactly 5'4" long, from the 6'-long 2 x 4s.

Then cut four rectangles, each 7" x 3", from the leftover plywood. Using the 2" screws, fasten two plywood rectangles to the tops of each of the 2 x 4s, forming a slot on each one (Fig. 8). Allow 3-1/2" of the plywood to extend above the 2 x 4s, and use three screws per plywood piece to make the attachment. Remember to bear forcefully on the screw while inserting it with the drill.

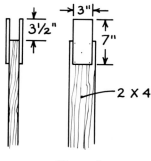

Figure 8

If the screws are difficult to insert using the electric drill, set them in position and tap them with a hammer to "bite" the ends into the wood. If the drill is stripping the screw head, use a smaller drill bit to make a pilot hole before installing the screw.

Now cut a 4'4" length from the 8'-long 2 x 4 and slip it into the plywood slots to fashion the top of the door frame (Fig. 9). The actual width of the door is 36". Set the 2 x 4 in place and measure so that the uprights are 36" apart.

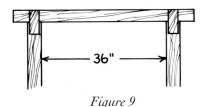

Figure 9

Make the door frame square by using a T-square or corner square. Another method of ensuring that your corners are 90 degrees is to measure the distance from one inside corner of the door frame

to the corner diagonally opposite; then match that distance with the distance between the other two diagonal corners. Set the frame square and screw the top of the door frame into the plywood slots, using three 2" screws on each side.

The remainder of the 8'-long 2 x 4 is for the bottom of the door frame, making a threshold. This piece is 3'7" long.

Set the threshold on its face (with the wider surface flat on the ground) on a flat surface. Then stand the door frame upon it and draw a line defining the exact placement of the vertical 2 x 4s as they sit upon the threshold (Fig. 10).

Cut out these two small rectangles by drilling holes in the inside corners (Fig. 10), then cutting out the sides with the jigsaw. Make the cuts exactly the size of the 2 x 4s that will be inserted into these slots.

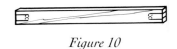

Figure 10

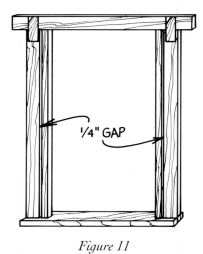

Figure 11

Spread wood-working glue on both surfaces to be connected and fit the upright 2 x 4s into the slots just cut. Check to make sure the angles of the door frame are square and screw the uprights into the threshold with 2" screws. Keep checking the angle of the uprights while the screws are being inserted because the boards shift easily until they are securely positioned.

Next you will install two 2 x 2 vertical struts within the door frame, allowing a 1/4" gap between each vertical strut and the door frame (Fig. 11). The purpose of the gap is to allow a space for the wall canvas to be pulled through and tied inside when pitching the yurt.

Measure and trim the ends of the 2 x 2 boards to fit inside the door frame. Screw them into place using one rectangular mending plate at the top of each 2 x 2 and one internal-angle mending plate at the bottom.

If the 2 x 2s are not quite as thick as the 2" edge of the 2 x 4s, just fasten the 2 x 2s so that they are both flush with one side of the 2 x 4s. This will be the front of your door frame. Since the hinges of the door are fastened to the 2 x 2 on the left, these 2 x 2s must be flush with the top and bottom of the door frame in order for the door to fit properly.

DOOR

To make the framework for the canvas-covered door, cut four 1 x 2s to fit the lengths shown in Fig. 12 and place them on a flat surface (up on a table is best for your back muscles). Position them with the corners in correct relationship with one another using the T-square or corner square.

A flat-angle mending plate is attached at the outer edges of each corner to hold the structure together. Since one mending plate is placed on the front and another on the back of each corner, you must position the plates to allow room for the screws on each side. Attach a 3" plate on one side and a 5" plate on the reverse side of each corner. Keep checking each corner's position

with the corner square as you attach the mending plates. Additionally, be very careful when inserting the screws so that you do not continue to drill after the screw is fully in place. This will crack the 1 x 2, and any 1 x 2s that are severely cracked must be replaced.

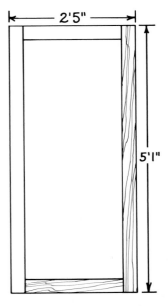

Figure 12

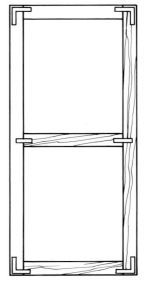

Figure 13

This door requires no special tools or woodworking skills to construct.

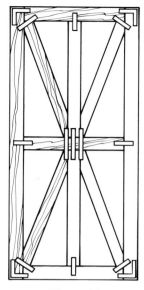

Figure 14

Now cut a 1 x 2 to fit across the middle of the door structure as shown in Fig. 13. Attach this piece into position with one 4" mending plate on each side of the door structure on both front and back, using four plates in total.

Cut the other support pieces of the door and attach them with mending plates as shown in Fig. 14. At each location, one plate goes on the front and one on the back of the door. Use the larger plates at the corners and in the center, where the diagonal spokes come together with the vertical pieces. The exact configuration of mending plates isn't important; attach them so that they make solid connections with each board.

Once the door structure is complete, staple a piece of canvas slightly larger than 2'5"' wide and 5'1" long to the front and back of the door. Fold under the edges and stretch the canvas so that it's taut against the framework.

Following the instructions on the box, attach the hinges to the door and door frame. Be careful to line up the hinges exactly in relationship with

one another. The hinges should be installed so that the door hangs slightly high because it will drop a bit after it has been standing vertically for a while.

The remaining 1 x 2s are used as molding to cover the gaps between the door and door frame. Measure, cut, and install the 1 x 2 molding pieces using 1-1/2" screws (Fig. 15). Install the molding on the back (inside) of the door frame.

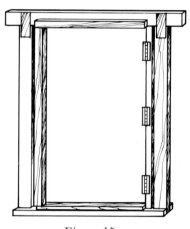

Figure 15

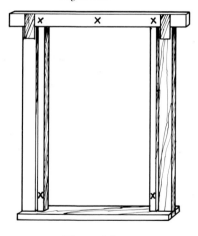

Figure 16

First install the molding piece on the bottom of the door frame. It will lie flat upon the threshold. Then install the other two pieces. Measure the exact length required for each strip and screw it into place. These tend to crack easily, so you must be extra careful.

Screw the gate-type door handles into place. The door handles often are placed at an angle to avoid bumping into the molding behind the door.

Now install the screen door catch (and slide latches, if desired), following the instructions on the package.

Attach five eyelet screws on the front side of the door frame as shown in Fig. 16. These are used to tie down the canvas with "drum strings" while pitching the yurt. To install the eyelet screws, just turn them by hand until they bite into the wood; then use a wrench to screw them in all the way.

Strips of the loop portion of hook and loop tape are fastened to the back (inside) of the door frame, along the vertical 2 x 2 inside struts. These strips are used to fasten the yurt liner securely into position later. Cut strips long enough to cover the entire length of the 2 x 2s, and staple them in place. The strip on the left, as you face the inside of the door frame, is stapled to the 1 x 2 molding piece that was previously installed.

The final task is to modify the two end khanas so that they can be bolted to the door frame, and to

drill holes into the door frame to accommodate the bolts that will attach the khanas.

Set the door frame against a wall or fence, with one khana on either side. Confirm that the khanas are positioned correctly by noting that the "B" marks are near the ground and the front sides of both khanas are facing you. (Remember the side with the bolt head is the front, and the side with the nut is the back or inside of the khana).

Now stretch one khana until it is the same height as the door frame. Mark it with a marking pen or chalk to indicate the places that must be cut with the jigsaw in order for the khana to fit the door frame at points G and H in Fig. 17. To complete the modification, you will have to unbolt the lattice at points G and H, make the cuts, sand the ends, then rebolt the lattice. Repeat this procedure with the other khana.

Finally, stretch the khanas on both sides of the door frame and mark the locations on the door frame where the holes must be drilled in order for the khanas to be bolted to the door frame (Fig. 17). The boards marked I and J in Fig. 17 must be shortened slightly to fit above the threshold.

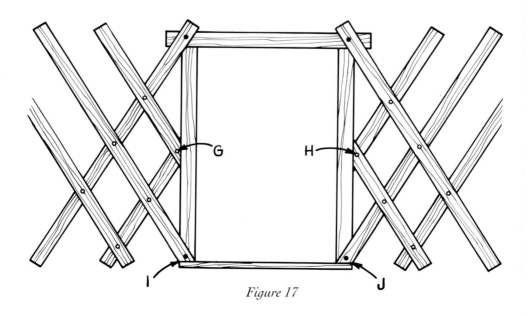

Figure 17

SEWING THE YURT CANVAS

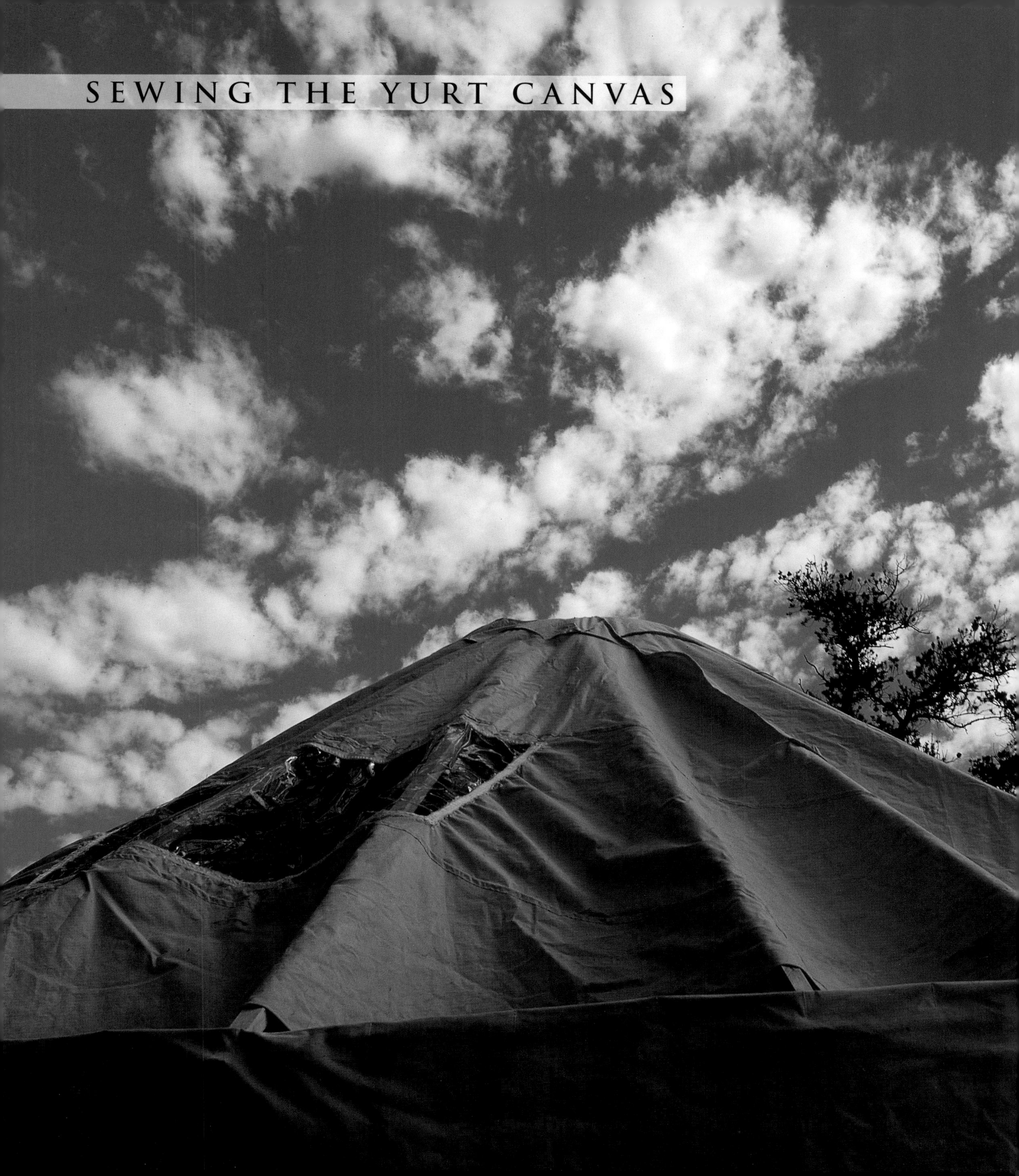

MATERIALS

The yurt canvas consists of four sections: door, walls, liner, and roof. The door is covered with canvas that is stapled on the front and back. A canvas wall covers the outer surface of the khanas, and a liner cloaks the inside lattice wall. The rafters and hub are protected by a canvas roof, which is sewn and fitted to the conical shape. (Recommended types of canvas and sewing thread are described in the chapter on materials and tools.) The material amounts required for each size yurt are listed in the table below.

If you plan to have windows in your yurt, you also will need mosquito netting, hook and loop tape, and a sheet of plastic for each one. Mosquito netting is used for the screen, and the hook and loop tape allows you to remove the plastic to "open" the window.

Various types of plastic can be used for windows, but the recommended material is polyvinyl chloride (PVC) that includes a clarifier and an ultraviolet inhibitor. Pressed sheets are better in quality than rolled goods. Sheets of 20-gauge

PVC generally can be obtained from the same supplier that provides the canvas for your yurt. The standard size plastic sheet used for a window is a rectangle 29" x 55".

If you install skylights, you won't need any netting or hook and loop tape, since these windows don't open, but you will need a tube of silicone sealant. Silicone helps keep water from penetrating around the edges of the plastic.

TOOLS

The most important tool needed for assembling the yurt canvas is a sewing machine, although the canvas also can be sewn by hand, if desired. The arrangement of your machine and work space for sewing a yurt canvas is described in the section called Setting Up to Sew, starting on page 9.

Other miscellaneous tools required include chalk, a fabric measuring tape, a carpenter's measuring tape at least as long as the diameter of your yurt, scissors, sewing machine oil, heavy-duty pins, and extra bobbins for your machine so that you can wind five or six at a time. When fit-

YURT CANVAS MATERIALS					
	Yurt Diameter				
	14'	18'	20'	24'	30'
Roof	39	60	69	109	148
Wall	29	38	42	52	67
Liner	29	38	42	52	67
Door	5	5	5	5	5
Total Canvas (in yards)	105	145	160	220	290
Nylon Webbing (in yards)	10	14	17	20	25
Rope (in feet)	200	300	400	500	600

ting the canvas roof to its frame, it is useful to have a few lengths of rope, one or two long poles, and a small ladder (for larger yurts only).

THE ROOF

The yurt roof consists of several strips of canvas of various lengths, which are sewn together into a shape resembling a pie minus one large slice. The assembled canvas is fit over the rafters and hub, then measured and sewn into a cone shape with a flattened tip (Fig. 1).

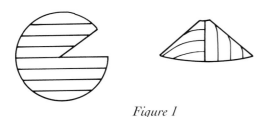

Figure 1

Refer at this time to the roof canvas pattern that corresponds with the yurt diameter desired (Figs. 2-6). Note that the strips on the top half of the pattern are shorter than those on the bottom. First you will sew together all of the strips for one half, then all of the strips for the other half. Finally, you will sew the two halves together. As you cut each strip, mark it with its identifying number on all four outside corners.

Skylights in the roof should be installed before sewing the roof canvas panels together. A skylight is a plastic sheet sewn into the roof in the desired location. Refer to the section on windows (page 90) for information on installing skylights.

The individual roof strips are sewn together using a modified welt seam, which involves two lines of stitching for each seam. The result is a strong seam that creates a shingle effect. When making these seams, care should be taken to ensure that they are sewn so that all of the "shingles" are properly aligned to shed the rain.

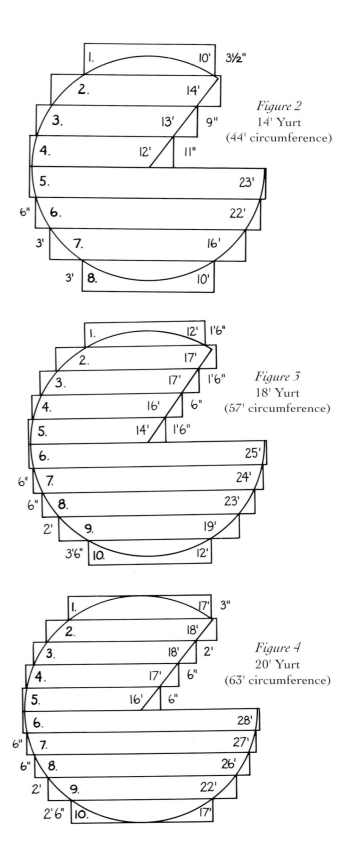

Figure 2
14' Yurt
(44' circumference)

Figure 3
18' Yurt
(57' circumference)

Figure 4
20' Yurt
(63' circumference)

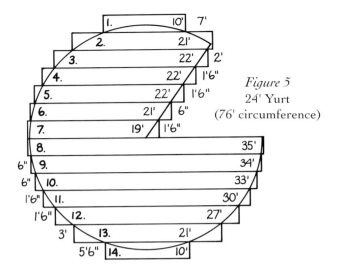

Figure 5
24' Yurt
(76' circumference)

Refer to the pattern to determine where to begin sewing. For example, the pattern may instruct you to begin sewing with strip 2 extending 1'8" beyond strip 1. Stitch 1/8" from the right edge of the top strip (Fig. 7). Do not push or pull the canvas through the machine; just guide the fabric to make a straight stitching line.

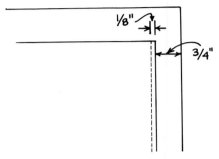

Figure 7

After you have completed the first sewing line, pull the bottom strip out from under the top one and spread it to your right. Fold the shorter strip at the seam so that the longer one now lies flat on top (Fig. 8). Sew a second seam line about 1/8" from the selvage edge of the longer strip. (You will need to fold the canvas lengthwise so that it can fit between the needle and the main body of the sewing machine.)

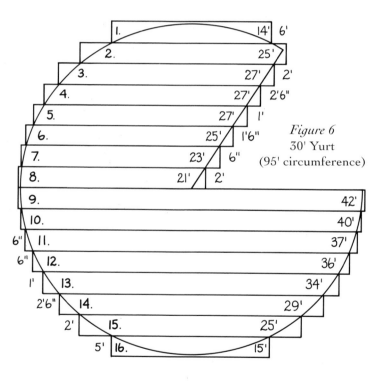

Figure 6
30' Yurt
(95' circumference)

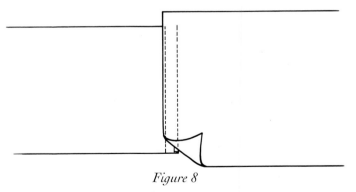

Figure 8

Notice that the stitching line on the right is flatter, and the one on the left is adjacent to a small ridge. This is the shingle, and the fact that it is on the shorter strip indicates that you are looking at the outside or right side of your canvas.

Cut strips 1 and 2 as specified in the appropriate pattern, and lay strip 1 on top of strip 2. The edges of the strips should face the machine, and the bulk of the fabric should rest to the left of the needle. Offset the top strip approximately 3/4" from the right edge of the bottom one.

Continue, adding each new strip underneath the one before it, until you have stitched together all the strips shown in the top half of the yurt roof canvas pattern. Refer each time to the chart to determine where to begin sewing one strip to the next.

The next step is to sew together all the strips for the bottom half of the yurt roof. Notice that all of these strips are longer than those on the top half. Beginning with the strip marked with the highest number (the shortest strip in the bottom half), cut this and the next highest numbered strip and sew them together. Sew the same welt seam, making the first stitching line with the longer strip on the bottom. Again refer to the chart to determine where to begin sewing.

Note that the figures for where to begin sewing are on the right side of the pattern for the upper half of the roof, while those same figures are on the left side for the lower half. This has to do with sewing the welt seam correctly to obtain the desired shingle effect.

Continue sewing every strip on the bottom half together. Each added strip will begin underneath and will be labeled with a number lower than the previously sewn strip.

After all of the strips have been sewn together, the two halves must be joined. To do this, place the top half of the roof canvas on top of the bottom half, with right sides together (Fig. 9). The bottom half lies to the left of the sewing machine, with its

longest strip closest to the machine. The highest numbered strip in the top half should be directly on top of the longest strip in the bottom half. To confirm that the right sides of the canvas are together, check to see that the flatter sides of the welt seams on both halves are facing inward.

Place the selvage edge of the bottom strip so that it extends 1/4" to the right of the strip on the top half (Fig. 10). Then stitch along this edge as shown in the figure. When the first line of stitching is complete, return the canvas to the starting position without unfolding the canvas underneath. Instead, fold the 1/4" overhang to the left and sew it down as shown in Fig. 10.

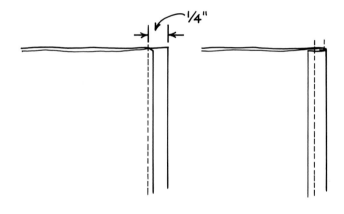

Figure 10

FITTING THE ROOF TO THE FRAME

Now that the roof is sewn together, you must fit it over an erected frame of proper proportions in order to determine exactly where you should sew the final seam that transforms the flat shape into a cone. This fitting also will enable you to dispense with canvas bulges and to cut the bottom edge of the canvas roof.

Find an area of flat, clean ground on which to set up the rafters and hub. Place the hub so that the

Wrong Side of Fabric

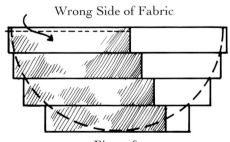

Figure 9

side with the cling-ons is facing down. The hub can be placed on a table, stool, or boxes to elevate it about 4' off the ground. Bolt each rafter into one of the cling-ons attached to the outer edge, and tighten the nuts by hand.

Using the metal tape measure, check the diameter of the circle formed by the rafters to determine how close it is to the desired diameter of your yurt. The diameter of the roof frame must be exactly equal to the diameter of the yurt you are making. For example, if you are constructing a 20' yurt, the rafters must be set up in a circle with an exact diameter of 20'. Be careful to avoid extending the bottoms of the rafters farther out than needed because they are very difficult to move back in to a smaller diameter.

Now toss the roof canvas, with the right side facing up, over the top of the frame structure. (The right side has the flatter "shingle" seams.) If you're making a large yurt, it will be easier if you tie ropes to the bottom edge of the canvas and pull the canvas over the top and into position with these ropes. Another helpful idea is to use poles to poke the canvas into position from inside the structure. Pull the canvas so that it generally covers the entire structure.

To transform your canvas roof into the shape of a cone that fits snugly over the roof frame, measure where to place the final vertical seam. Tug and shift the canvas around until it is in the best position; then pin the seam.

One side of the seam is a selvage edge, and the other consists of the ends of several canvas strips. After you have determined where to mark and pin the seam, you will trim the uneven side.

Don't be concerned if there's a bulge of canvas in one area after most of the roof canvas has been gathered up to fit snugly around the frame. This is normal and will be fixed in a later step. Also,

while you are pulling the canvas into position for the final vertical seam, keep in mind that you will need to have 8" to 10" of canvas extending beyond the ends of the rafters all around the bottom edge of the yurt roof.

When you have jockeyed the canvas into the best possible position, mark a seam line with chalk. Then cut off the excess, taking care not to cut off more than you should. Don't be concerned that there seems to be too much canvas at the very top of the canvas roof, for this also will be fixed in a later step. After cutting off the excess canvas, pin the seam into position with heavy-duty pins and mark your stitching line with chalk.

With scissors in hand, go under the roof and poke the upper half of your body out through the top area of the seam that has just been pinned. There is no need to cut an opening, but you will have to undo a few pins in order to make a large enough opening.

The next task is to cut away the canvas that is currently above the hub. (To do this on larger yurts, you will need to use a ladder.) This canvas will be replaced with a flat circle of canvas the size of your hub.

In order to make the circular cut as neat as possible, fold and press the canvas where it tends to overlap (Fig. 11). This is called making a dart.

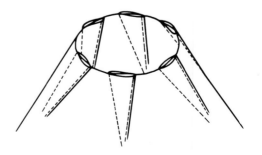

Figure 11

For a neater finish, make several small darts rather than a few large ones. You may want to secure them with pins before cutting. Then mark the circle approximately 2" smaller than the circumference of the hub and cut.

After cutting the circle, adjust the darts so that the canvas fits snugly on the frame. Fold and press the excess canvas, making it lie down as neatly as possible, and pin the darts into position for sewing. In addition, mark the edges of each dart with chalk. This is necessary because the pins may be pulled out of position while you're moving the canvas and because you may forget where you need to sew after you've returned to the machine with this huge mass of canvas.

Now remove the excess canvas from around the bottom of the roof. Measure 10" beyond the circumference of the yurt, as defined by the ends of the rafters, and place a chalk mark every 8" or so. Then cut off any extra canvas.

You may find that you have an area where the canvas comes up a bit short. Simply proceed by writing—directly on the canvas with chalk—how much more canvas is needed in that area. When you return to the sewing machine, add the patch, making a welt seam to match the others. Once the patch is added, simply cut off any excess.

Once you've finished these steps for fitting the canvas roof, disassemble the structure and return to the sewing machine.

First sew the final vertical seam, following the same basic procedure used to join the two halves of the canvas roof (Fig. 10, page 87), but with one modification. Place the selvage edge on top and the cut edge on the bottom, offsetting it about 1/2". In order to prevent the cut edge from unraveling in the future, turn under about 1/4" before adding the second stitching line. Begin sewing this seam at the top of the yurt roof and

end at the bottom. It may be necessary to trim away more excess canvas to make the seam fit exactly along the chalk line and ensure a snug fit.

Next sew the darts where they have been marked with chalk. First sew down one edge, then the other to secure both sides of each dart (Fig. 11).

Now cut a circle of canvas exactly the same size as your hub. Sew this circle to the opening at the top of the roof canvas, using the same seam just described. Place the roof canvas on the bottom and the flat circle on top, offsetting it 1/2". Remember to fold over the cut edge before making the second line of stitching so that the ragged edge won't unravel later. If the opening at the top of the roof is somewhat larger than the circle of canvas, lightly gather it as you sew the first line of stitching.

After these steps have been completed, and any necessary patches added, sew a hem around the bottom edge of the roof canvas. Fold the edge twice and sew it once all the way around.

PEG LOOPS

The final step in assembling the roof canvas is to make and attach the peg loops. These are placed every 18" around the roof, about 10" up from the bottom edge. Cut two squares of canvas, one 4" x 4" and the other 2" x 2", and one 5"-long piece of nylon webbing for each peg loop.

Hem the outer edges of all the canvas squares by folding over once and sewing once. Now sew one of the nylon webbing strips to the back of each 2" x 2" square, making a loop with the webbing strip. To complete each peg loop, sew one 2" x 2" square (complete with looped webbing strip) onto the front of each 4" x 4" square (Fig. 12).

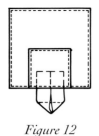

Figure 12

Measure 10" up from the hemmed edge on the outside of the roof canvas and mark a chalk line all the way around. Then sew one completed peg loop every 18" along the marked line.

WALLS

The width of your canvas determines how you must proceed with making the walls of your yurt. If you're using canvas that is 3' wide, then you must sew two strips together to make the desired 6' wall. With 5'-wide canvas, you must cut and sew a 1' strip along the entire edge. If you want to include windows in the canvas walls of your yurt, you must install them before sewing any strips together.

Determine the length of canvas needed for your wall from the measurements given in the table on page 84. The walls are a few feet longer than the circumference of the yurt to allow some extra fabric for securing the ends of the canvas walls to the door frame.

If you're using canvas that is 5' wide, you will need one length equal to the circumference of the yurt plus a few feet, and you will need a second length equal to the total length of your wall divided by five. The second length is cut into 1' strips and the strips are sewn together lengthwise to add to your wall for the desired 6' height.

The canvas wall is attached to the yurt frame by means of pockets sewn along the top of the canvas. Starting at one end, fold over the top edge of the canvas 1-1/2" and pin it down in this manner for several feet at a time. The pockets are made by sewing vertical lines every 10" all along the top of the canvas wall.

Now hem the ends of the canvas wall by folding over twice and sewing once. To fasten the wall to the yurt frame, three 3' lengths of webbing are sewn to each end of the canvas wall in the locations shown in Fig. 13. Allow the end of the webbing to overlap the canvas by several inches for security. Burn the free end of each length of webbing and sew the other end to the canvas so that it's turned under and won't unravel.

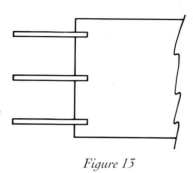

Figure 13

WINDOWS

A yurt window is made using mosquito netting for the screen and a sheet of plastic for the actual window. The netting is sewn into the window opening in the canvas, and the plastic window is installed with hook and loop tape, which allows it to be removed easily.

Once you've decided where you want to place your windows, spread that area of the canvas on a flat surface. Windows generally are placed in the top half of the wall, in a position that best utilizes the potential sunlight and possibilities for viewing the landscape. Some people like to make vertical windows rather than horizontal ones. Vertical windows must be installed after assembling the complete 6' wall, unless you're working with 5'-wide canvas and add the 1' strip either under or over the window.

Lay the plastic window on the canvas in the desired position and mark around the outer edges

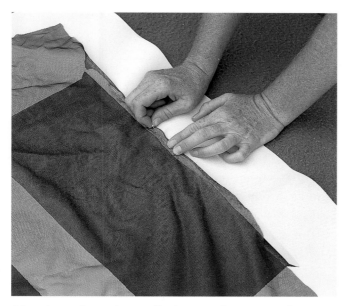

Mosquito netting makes an effective screen for a yurt window.

of the rectangle. Remove the window and set it aside. Now mark a second rectangle 2" inside the first. Carefully following the lines, cut out the inside rectangle of canvas. The rectangle that is cut out of the canvas will become the flap over the window, so cut only on the marked lines.

On each of the four corners of the rectangular opening in the canvas wall, make a cut about 1" long (Fig. 14). Then fold under all four edges of the rectangle. Cut a piece of mosquito netting just slightly larger than the size of the window and fold the edges of the netting under the corresponding folded edges of the rectangular window opening (Fig. 15). This results in a folded edge for both the netting and the canvas. After pinning it, sew the netting in place.

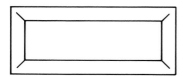

Figure 14

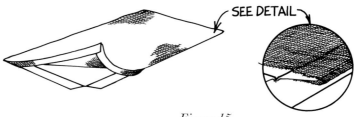

Figure 15

Now sew a strip of the hook portion of hook and loop tape around the outer edge of the plastic window. Then lay the window on the mosquito netting and mark the outline of the window onto the netting with chalk. Sew the loop portion of the hook and loop tape to the netting, just inside the mark. The hook and loop tape allows you to remove or replace the plastic window over the mosquito netting as needed.

The rectangular piece of canvas that was cut out of the wall can be pieced with small strips of canvas to make the window flap. The flap should be large enough to cover the window and have 5" to spare all around. First sew a 7" wide strip of canvas along the top of the rectangle; then add a second strip of canvas 7" wide on one side. After adding the strips to the rectangle, sew a hem around the entire flap by simply folding the edge over twice and sewing once. The seams and hem should take up about 2".

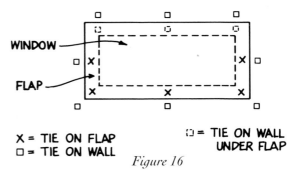

Figure 16

Now lay the flap over the window and mark the locations of the ties, as shown in Fig. 16. At the same time, mark the yurt wall to indicate where the top of the flap should be attached above the window. Note that the flap is attached between the two rows of ties across the top of the window. This allows the flap to be rolled up and tied in place.

For each window and flap, cut ten nylon webbing ties 9" long and six ties 12" long. The longer ties are used across the top of the window. Seal one end of each tie by burning it in a flame. Now sew the ties on all the marked locations, both on the flap and around the window itself. Sew the canvas window flap (between the two rows of longer ties) above the window by sewing along the top edge of the flap.

Much larger expanses of mosquito netting can be sewn into your yurt wall using the same procedure. During storms, cover the openings with large sheets of plastic or canvas that are framed with hook and loop tape. Another option is to sew the plastic sheets directly into the canvas walls (see Skylights, below). These windows can be as large as you wish and covered, when desired, with canvas framed with hook and loop tape.

SKYLIGHTS

Because they don't have screens, skylights are simpler to construct than windows. They consist of plastic sheets sewn directly into the canvas and sealed with silicone.

Determine the desired location for one or more skylights by looking at the yurt roof canvas pattern on paper. Keep in mind that the flat pie shape will be transformed into a cone (and that the skylight will be angled relative to the ground). Remember too that the roof is designed so that when the yurt is pitched, you can easily maneuver the canvas around to place the skylights in different positions for different seasons.

Draw the skylights directly onto the pattern (Fig. 17). It's easier to locate each skylight within a single strip; otherwise you will have to sew

Figure 17

two strips together to get the proper expanse of canvas in which to install your skylight. Once you've determined the precise location desired on the pattern paper, cut out the corresponding length of canvas and mark its identifying numbers on each of the four corners.

Cut a sheet of plastic the desired size for your skylight and lay the plastic rectangle directly on the strip of canvas in the chosen location. Carefully draw a chalk line around the skylight. Remove the plastic and draw a second chalk line 2-1/2" inside the first.

Following the lines exactly, cut out the inside rectangle. Then make 1" diagonal cuts at each corner (see Fig. 14, page 91). Fold back the edges 1/4" and again at 1" to create a smooth unraveled edge and pin the folds in place. Lay the plastic skylight on top and attach it with two lines of stitching (Fig. 18). After the whole roof

Figure 18

has been completed, apply a silicone sealant to the edges of the skylight to prevent rain from leaking into the yurt.

LINER

The liner consists of a 6'-tall canvas wall that is installed inside the yurt. Construct the liner so that it's equal in length to the circumference of your yurt minus 3'. This is because the door is 3' wide, and the liner begins and ends on either side of the door.

If you have windows, you probably will want to make the liner in sections that allow you to fold back the liner at each side of each window. Then the window can be exposed when desired and covered with the liner when necessary. If you live in an extremely cold climate, you have the option of installing liner canvas above and below each window. Simply cut canvas pieces to fit these locations; then hem the edges and sew nylon ties to the corners. Tie these pieces to the lattice wall.

Along the top edge of the liner, nylon webbing ties are placed every 3'. Cut each tie 9" long and seal both ends by passing them through a flame. Fold each tie in half and sew it to the liner, making a double tie that is 4-1/2" long on each side.

The ends of the liner are attached to the door frame using hook and loop tape. This allows you to secure the liner firmly to the door frame, helping to make the yurt snug in cold weather. Sew a length of the hook portion of the tape on the back side of each end of the liner. (The loop portion of the tape was installed when making the door frame.)

DOOR

The canvas portion of the door consists of two pieces of fabric cut to fit, then stapled onto the door structure. Generally, the canvas is attached to the door before the hinges, latches, and door handle are installed. If you haven't already done so, cut two pieces of canvas, each slightly larger than 2'5" wide and 5'1" long. As you staple it to the door, fold under the edges and pull the canvas taut.

When cutting the canvas for the door, you also can add a window if desired. Just follow the procedure previously described for sewing windows in the walls or for installing a skylight in the roof, but use smaller pieces of plastic and mosquito netting.

MATERIALS AND TOOLS

To assemble your yurt, you'll need all of the components that you have constructed so far—the lattice sections (khanas), rafters, hub, door, and door frame—and those that you have sewn— roof canvas, wall, and liner. Additional materials include a small-diameter nylon rope in a length equal to four times the circumference of your yurt, a 3/16"-diameter steel cable equal in length to the circumference of your yurt, a 3/16" turnbuckle, and four appropriately sized clamps. Also needed are four 1/4" x 3" bolts with 1/4" nuts for attaching the khanas to the door frame and several 1/4" x 2" hex-head bolts with 1/4" nuts (one per rafter plus enough to bolt all of the khanas together).

Necessary tools include a measuring tape that is long enough to measure the yurt diameter, one or two long poles (the same length as the rafters), a small wrench for the clamps, and a wrench for the 1/4" nuts and bolts. If your yurt is 24' or larger, or if you have a site with a steep bank, at least one ladder is advisable.

If you're installing your yurt on the ground, you'll need one stake for every 6' of your circumference, plus four additional stakes. Choose stakes that will function in the type of soil that you have. For example, if the soil is loose, use very long stakes; if the soil is hard, use slim, sharply pointed stakes. A sledge hammer or an equivalent tool is needed to pound the stakes into the ground.

For a deck-mounted yurt, boat hardware is the best means for securing the structure. Purchase enough hardware to place one tie-down every 6' around the circumference of the yurt, plus four additional pieces. You'll need a drill and wood screws to install the hardware.

ORIENTING THE YURT

After preparing the site and making a floor, as described in the chapter on site selection, determine how you wish to orient your yurt. Traditionally, the Mongols erected their yurts with the doors facing south. Likewise, the only opening in a circle of yurts was to the south. Apparently the southerly orientation was based upon the belief that the Mongols' enemies would most likely come from that direction. I suggest you face your door in the most convenient direction and position your windows for the best views of the beauty around you.

ASSEMBLING THE FRAME

Once you've decided how to situate your yurt, you will need at least four people for its assembly. Begin by having one person hold the door frame in the designated place while another person positions one of the modified khanas alongside it. Establish the correct orientation of the khana so that its holes match up with those in the door frame. For example, the khana that is modified

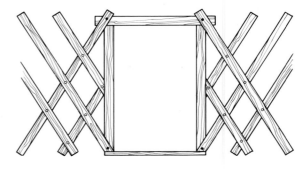

Figure 1

to fit on the left side of the door (as you face them both from the outside) should have the bolt heads facing out and the nuts facing in and should conform to the pattern shown in Fig. 1.

The easiest way to bolt the first khana in place is to stretch it out straight away from the door frame. You can bend the khana into a circular shape later. Pull the khana out so that its height approximately matches that of the door frame. If you have sufficient flat ground, the fully extended khana stands up by itself. Be very careful not to pinch your fingers while moving it.

Using the 1/4" x 3" bolts, attach the ends of the lattice to the front side of the door frame. Don't tighten the nuts against the door frame; these should be loose enough to allow the khana plenty of room to bend.

Repeat this procedure to attach the second modified khana on the other side of the door frame.

Now bolt the remaining khanas into position to form a complete circle. In order for the khanas to match up compatibly, the bottom of each lattice section (marked with a "B") must rest on the ground and the front side (with bolt heads) must face out.

Be careful not to place too much stress on the khanas that are attached directly to the door frame. They can't bend as freely as the others due to the inflexibility of the door frame. Just be aware of this and begin bending the lattice into a circular shape a few feet away from the door frame.

Don't be concerned at first about placing the wall lattice in the correct diameter for your yurt; just get the khanas bolted together properly. You may need to add or remove a lattice piece or two to get the khanas to fit together. This will have no ill effect upon the finished yurt.

Once the khanas are bolted together, measure and adjust the circular lattice so that it conforms exactly to the correct diameter. Set the diameter by measuring with the tape from the door to the back and from side to side. To move a khana, stand inside the yurt with your back to the lat-

tice, grab hold with both hands, and use your body weight to push the wall back or pull it forward into position.

Next place the steel cable around the top of the wall, laying the cable into the V shapes formed by the tops of the lattice pieces (Fig. 2). At the doorway, the cable fits in between the plywood rectangles on top of the door frame.

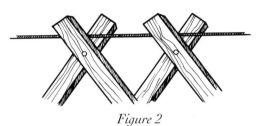

Figure 2

When it's tightened and secured with the turnbuckle and cable clamps, the cable forms a tension ring. Start with the turnbuckle in its most open position. After feeding two clamps onto one end of the cable, pass the end through the loop at one end of the turnbuckle and return it through the clamps. Repeat with the other end of the cable (Fig. 3).

Figure 3

Two people are needed to remove the slack along the full length of the cable. Beginning directly across from the turnbuckle, each person should pull the cable and take up the slack all the way around to the turnbuckle. (This is easier if you position the turnbuckle between the tops of two khanas.) After the slack has been taken out, tighten the clamps on the cable and close the turnbuckle. This procedure leaves the cable with the desired amount of tension, which will be equalized by the rafters pressing down on it. If the cable were any tighter, it would cause the lattice walls to creep inward.

Begin the assembly process by bolting the first two khanas to the door frame.

Continue bolting khanas together until you have a complete circle.

Measure to confirm that the diameter of the circle is correct.

Place the steel cable tension ring along the top of the lattice wall.

Bring the hub inside the yurt and place it on a box, crate, or bench in the middle. It's easier to work with if the hub is 3' or so off the ground. The hub is placed with the "arms" of the cling-on facing down.

Now bring all the rafters inside the yurt and fan them out around the hub. Place the ends with the holes near the hub and let the notched ends extend through the bottom of the lattice.

Bolt one of the rafters into each cling-on around the hub, tightening the nuts by hand. Washers aren't needed.

At least three strong people are needed now to lift the notched ends of three rafters, spaced equal distances apart, while a fourth person lifts the hub. Watching each other carefully, raise the hub and rafters in unison, keeping the hub as horizontal as possible. As soon as it's possible, set the three rafters upon the steel cable. Push the top of the lattice wall out as needed to help position the notched rafter onto the cable.

After the first three have been placed, lift the remaining rafters and set the notched ends onto the steel cable. Be on the watch for falling rafters; until they're all settled and in place, they

Bolt the rafters onto the hub, tightening the nuts by hand.

Set the notched end of each rafter onto the cable tension ring.

have a tendency to slip out at the notched end and swing free. If you've drilled holes across the rafter notches, slip a small nail through each one as you set the rafter onto the cable. This precaution will keep the rafters from slipping.

Make sure that each rafter is lined up properly by walking around the yurt, standing near the notched end of each rafter, and looking up to the hub. A properly placed rafter comes straight down from the hub. If a rafter is out of line and its cling-on is severely bent, move the rafter and bend the cling-on back into shape with a pair of pliers. Adjust the position of only one rafter at a time. It's not wise to have several people changing rafter positions at once.

When you move the notched end of a rafter, push the top of the wall lattice out (while standing inside the yurt, facing the lattice) and reposition the rafter as needed. If it's difficult to undo a rafter, have one person push the top of the wall with both hands while another person moves the rafter. Although they're a bit widely spaced, the rafters adjacent to the door are to be positioned on either side of the door.

In the larger yurts (24' and 30'), at least one ladder is necessary to raise the hub and place the

first three rafters. The height of the hub is 11' for a 24' yurt and 13' for a 30' yurt, so you'll need a ladder that is 10' or 12' tall.

The sheer number and length of the rafters in the larger yurts make the whole roof frame quite heavy. One way to manage this is to have a crowd of helpers. Position one or two at the notched end of each rafter and have one or two others raise the hub while each is walking up a ladder. (Be sure to station someone at the foot of each ladder to stabilize it while someone else is climbing.) The people holding the rafters should provide some support to the hub as it is being lifted. Work slowly and synchronize your movements. As soon as possible, position the rafters on the cable. Then resettle them individually as needed.

Keep in mind that the cling-ons will bend if strained, but they're easily returned to the correct position with pliers.

Another method for handling larger yurts is to bolt only four rafters to the hub to start. You can raise the hub with far fewer people this way. Attach the four rafters equal distances apart in order to give the hub the best possible foundation. Then raise the hub using a ladder as outlined in the first method. After the first four

Insert one end of the wall canvas through the gap in the door frame and fasten it to the lattice.

Wrap the rest of the canvas around the wall, slipping the pockets onto the tops of the khanas.

rafters have been placed on the steel cable, some-one must climb the ladder, which is placed under the hub, and bolt additional rafters in place, one at a time. This is accomplished by having the person on the ground pass the hub end of the rafter up to the person on the ladder.

In order to align each rafter with a cling-on so that it can be bolted easily, the notched end of the rafter should extend through one of the spaces along the bottom edge of the wall lattice. When the rafter is lined up correctly, you will find that the bolt pops right into place. It's better to take the time to reposition the notched end of the rafter than to try forcing the bolt through the hub end of the rafter. Continue bolting rafters in, allowing them to dangle freely until they're all in place. Then set all the notched ends onto the cable (watching for slipped and loose rafters as you go), aligning them with the cling-ons at the hub. Finally, tighten the nuts at the cling-ons.

INSTALLING THE CANVAS

Now it's time to install the canvas wall. Making sure that the outside of the wall is facing out, pull one end of the canvas through the gap

between the two vertical pieces in the door frame. Then fold the canvas back from the door and pull it tight. Using the nylon ties that are sewn to the ends of the wall canvas, fasten one end of the canvas to the inside of the lattice. Attach the rest of the wall all the way around the yurt by slipping the pockets, which are sewn intermittently along the top of the wall canvas, onto the tops of the khanas. When you reach the doorway with the other end of the canvas, secure it as you did the first end.

The next step is to place the canvas roof over the frame. Pull the entire roof canvas up onto the edge of the frame at any location. The outside of the roof canvas has the flatter side of the welt seam and has peg loops around the outer edge.

For larger yurts, it helps to tie two ropes to peg loops on opposite sides. Using one or two extra poles, push the canvas up from inside the yurt. Poke the pole into the canvas at its highest point and maneuver the canvas higher until it rolls over the top of the roof. Meanwhile, two people can pull on the ropes and help position the edges of the canvas around the circumference of the yurt.

On smaller yurts the canvas can be manipulated with poles and by hand; ropes are unnecessary.

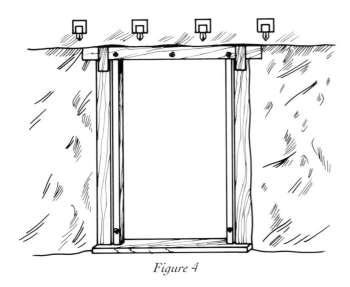

Figure 4

The circle of canvas in the very center of the roof should lie directly above the hub, and the main body of the roof should be pulled down evenly around the sides.

With people standing around the yurt, approximately evenly spaced, pull the roof around into the desired position. Position your skylights (if any) and be sure that the peg loops above the door are correctly placed. Two of the peg loops should be spaced evenly between the three eyelet screws in the top of the door frame as shown in Fig. 4.

Don't be concerned if the hub isn't sitting perfectly flat. This will straighten out as you stake the canvas into place. If the hub is still slightly askew when the yurt has been completely assembled, simply go inside and push up on the hub from underneath with a pole, jockeying it into the correct position. Once you push it into place, tighten the nuts again on each rafter to secure the hub.

Now stake the roof canvas in place. Tie a piece of rope, 9' to 10' in length, to each of four evenly spaced peg loops on the roof. Secure the other end of each rope to the ground using stakes or to your deck using boat tie-down hardware.

If you have a deck that is the same size as your yurt, you can fold the canvas wall underneath the deck's edge and fasten with it with dry wall screws. Otherwise, the canvas can be fastened the standard way—a method called *stringing the drum*.

Left: Pull the roof canvas up onto one edge of the roof frame; then jockey the canvas into place.

Opposite page: Arrange the roof canvas so that the peg loops are placed correctly.

To anchor the "drum strings" that hold down the roof and wall canvas, tie one end of the long nylon rope to the eyelet screw at the bottom right side of the door frame. Holding the rope about 8" off the ground, bring it all the way around the yurt and, after cutting the rope, tie the other end to the eyelet screw on the opposite side of the bottom of the door frame.

Secure the drum string anchor rope by pounding a stake into the ground every 6' around the yurt and tying a length of nylon rope between the anchor rope and each stake. Position the stakes

just outside your rain trench around the yurt. If your yurt is mounted on a deck, use the tie-down hardware for this purpose.

From the remaining length of nylon rope, cut a piece about 20' long and tie one end to the same eyelet screw at the bottom right of the door frame. Bring the other end of the rope up to the first peg loop to your right along the roof canvas edge, then down to the drum string anchor rope. Continue to "string the drum" until you run out of rope. Then tie the end (after pulling with all your strength) to a peg loop or to the anchor

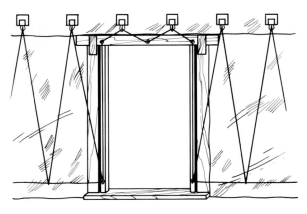

Figure 5

rope. Cut another length of rope (about 20' or as long as you wish) and continue zigzagging it from peg loops to the anchor rope completely around the circumference of the yurt.

When you've gone all the way around the yurt and are back to the door frame, thread the rope through the eyelet screw on the bottom left side of the door frame, up the vertical strut, and zigzag it through the eyelet screws and peg loops near the top of the door frame (Fig. 5). Then continue the rope back down the vertical strut on the right side of the door frame and tie it off on the eyelet screw at the bottom.

The bottom edge of the roof canvas can be left as it is or folded under for a neater look. The roof canvas above the door probably will need to be folded under in order for the door to open and shut properly.

Fasten the liner to the steel tension cable using the ties along the top edge of the liner panels. Complete the liner installation by fastening together the hook and loop tape at the ends of the liner to the matching tape on the door frame.

STAYING DRY

The only place where water might come into a yurt

is around the bottom. Most of the excess water can be directed away from the yurt by means of a rain trench. The size of the trench required varies according to the amount of rain, type of soil, and other conditions. In general, a trench 4" to 6" deep is sufficient for most situations, but it's better to err on the side of caution than to have to deal with a soggy mess. Additional steps that you can take vary according to how you assemble your yurt.

If your yurt is on the ground and you're in the midst of a rainy season, you can prevent the water from seeping in and protect the canvas around the bottom from mildewing by putting a plastic rain skirt around the bottom. To do this, cut a piece of plastic that is 2' wide and equal in length to the circumference of your yurt (minus the 3' door). Slip the top edge of this plastic underneath and behind the canvas wall and place the bottom edge into the trench. The drum strings will hold the plastic rain skirt in place.

If you build a deck the same size as the yurt and raise it slightly off the ground, then you can secure the outer wall under and around the deck. Unless you have a heavy flood that brings water up to the level of your deck, you should have no problem with water.

If your deck extends beyond the edge of the yurt, then you will have to take some precautions to keep standing water from soaking through the canvas wall of the yurt. One way to keep the floor dry is to build your deck in two layers. Construct a main deck exactly the same size as the yurt and build a subdeck underneath that extends out beyond the main deck. Another technique is to attach 2' lengths of 1 x 2 lumber along the inside edge of the bottom of the yurt and to seal the boards to the deck with silicone. The sealant is easy to apply with an inexpensive applicator available at a hardware store.

Bender board is another useful material for making your yurt water tight. This is a soft, flexible siding material made from rough redwood that is commonly used for creating edges in garden beds because it can be curved as desired. Bender board is 1/4" thick and 4" wide, and it comes in lengths ranging from 8' to 16'.

Place the bender board around the outside of the yurt wall all along the bottom and hold it in place with the drum string anchor rope. A silicone sealant placed around the bottom of the board will help make it impermeable.

As each khana is disconnected, it can be compressed into a compact unit.

DISASSEMBLING THE YURT

Start with the basics: remove everything from inside the yurt, take down the liner, and remove all of the ropes that hold the canvas in place.

Now take down the roof canvas. The easiest method for doing this is to guide the canvas with poles while standing inside the yurt. Once the canvas slides over the top of the hub, you can pull it down the side and away from the frame.

Remove the wall canvas by untying either side at the door frame and lifting the pockets off the lattice framework.

Fold all of the canvas sections and set them aside. Be careful that the canvas is completely dry before storing it; if it's even slightly damp, there's a good chance it will mildew.

To remove the rafters and hub, begin by lifting all but three or four rafters off the tension cable. This is done by pushing out the top of the lattice wall and pushing up the end of the rafter. The remaining few rafters should be spaced equal distances apart so that they continue to support the hub. The released rafters will pivot and hang down from the hub into the center of the yurt.

With a person positioned at the bottom of each of the remaining rafters, everyone simultaneously should lift the rafters up and away from the tension cable. Once all of the rafters have been released from the top of the wall, lower them until you can reach the hub. Then remove the bolts and nuts that connect the rafters to the hub.

To remove the steel cable tension ring, loosen the turnbuckle and remove the clamps from one end. After lifting it off the lattice wall, coil the cable into a circle for storage.

Begin disconnecting the khanas at a point opposite the door where two sections of lattice come together. You will find it easier to remove the nuts and bolts if you position the work area in as straight a line as possible. Remove only as many nuts and bolts as are necessary to disconnect the khanas; don't disassemble the structure into individual boards unless necessary.

Continue disconnecting the khanas from one another until you have just one section connected to each side of the door. Have someone hold the door to steady the structure as you straighten the lattice and remove the final nuts and bolts.

Living with a CIRCULAR SHELTER

HEATING

Several factors should be considered when deciding how to heat your new shelter. These include cost, availability of the appropriate combustible materials, and convenience. Firewood may be abundant, but it must be replenished frequently to keep a fire burning. The size of your shelter and whether it is a tipi or a yurt also should be taken into account. A larger yurt has plenty of room for a wood stove, but a smaller tipi may feel too cramped.

OPEN FIRES

Open fires are much more satisfactory in tipis than in yurts. This is because the tall, conical shape of the tipi provides a natural chimney for the smoke. This effect is further enhanced by the liner. With a liner installed, the movement of cooler air up the outside wall draws the smoke up and out. Furthermore, a tipi has smoke flaps that can be adjusted according to weather conditions to help ventilate the structure.

In order to have a fire in a yurt, you must cut a hole in the hub and the canvas above it to allow the smoke to escape. To prevent rain from coming in, install a flap of canvas that covers the opening. This can be made to sit up from the roof if you want to have a fire burning during the rain.

The best way to learn about fire is through experience, although there are some steps you can take to improve the quality of your fire. The first is to locate the fire where smoke will ventilate best. In a tipi, place the fire pit just in front of the very center of the floor. The best location in a yurt is the exact center.

A stone hearth helps to create a hot and smokeless fire. This can be as simple as placing a ring of stones on the bare earth or as solid as building a raised hearth of stones and mortar.

To provide more oxygen for the fire to burn better, you can bury a pipe from the fire pit to a location outside your shelter. Just be careful where you place the outside end of the pipe to avoid flooding the fire in a heavy rain. It's also helpful to have a bellows or blowpipe for those times when the fire needs a little coaxing to get it going.

WOOD STOVES

Wood stoves work very well in tipis and yurts. They're an effective means of providing warmth, and either structure is small enough to be heated easily, especially with the liner installed for insulation. Burning hardwood in an airtight wood stove provides the maximum heat and efficiency.

The easiest way to install a wood stove in a tipi is to extend the stovepipe up from the stove and let the smoke find its way out through the flaps. In a yurt, it's possible to have an open hole in the roof, which allows you to have a freestanding stovepipe inside, but this tends to be a smokey proposition, since the yurt doesn't draw as well as the tipi.

A smoke-free, rain-free approach is to direct the stovepipe out through the wall of the tipi or yurt. The stovepipe runs vertically above the stove, horizontally through the wall, then vertically again outside. A thimble provides insulation between the stovepipe and the wall of your shelter, and a spark arrester placed at the top of the stovepipe prevents accidental fires. These devices and the other necessary hardware can be purchased from a wood stove supplier.

For a tipi, install the thimble in a piece of plywood. Then attach a 2 x 2 to the top and bottom of the plywood and lash the unit to two of the tipi poles (Fig. 1).

A snow fence helps shelter the tip from blowing snow.

COURTESY TOM SLATER

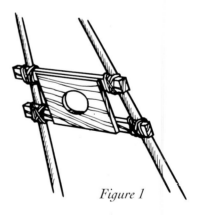

Figure 1

Before placing a stove in your tipi or yurt, check with the stove manufacturer (or your local fire department) to determine the clearances you should maintain between the components of the stove and the walls of your shelter (Fig. 2). Also confirm the height needed for the stovepipe outside the structure; this is usually measured relative to the height of your roof.

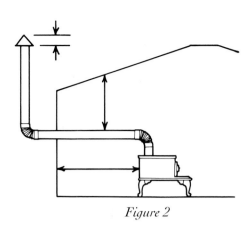

Figure 2

PROPANE AND KEROSENE HEATERS

There are several types of both these heaters on the market. The catalytic heaters are more efficient than regular types because they recycle and burn their own fumes. They're odorless and very quiet. For safety purposes, units with automatic shutoff valves are preferable. With either type of heater—kerosene or propane—a relatively small amount of fuel lasts for many hours.

PASSIVE SOLAR HEAT

The simplest method for obtaining passive solar heat is to install plastic windows in the canvas cover of your tipi or yurt. Position the plastic windows so that they're in prime locations for maximum sun absorption. The lower angle of the winter sun allows more energy to come into your shelter during the months when it's most needed. Plastic windows can be as large as you wish, and shades made of light-colored fabrics can be sewn onto the canvas to keep your living area from getting too hot on warm days.

In a yurt, it's possible to have whole sections of wall made primarily of window plastic. A brick floor absorbs the heat from the sun during the day and radiates the heat back into your yurt at night.

Buried in snow up to the stove pipe!

COURTESY TOM SLATER

The snow fence was no match for this blizzard.

COURTESY TOM SLATER

To receive sufficient sunlight in the woods, these photovoltaic panels are raised high above the ground.

COURTESY TOM SLATER

In an open spot, solar panels can be mounted on the ground.

COURTESY TOM SLATER

In colder climates, the window areas can be made more efficient by layering two, three, or even four plastic windows together with 1" of dead air space between each one for insulation. This makes a formidable barrier against cold.

Many other, more ambitious approaches using solar energy have been developed and are available for you to try. A number of sources of information on solar products are listed on page 122.

INSULATION

No matter what your method of heating, you will have a warmer shelter if it's insulated. The type and amount of insulation needed depends upon the severity of your climate.

One method for insulating a tipi or yurt is to install two to four layers of liner canvas. For best results, separate the layers by about 1". To do this, position boards around the perimeter of the floor and tack the bottoms of the liners the appropriate distances apart. At the top of the wall, fasten the liners to the liner rope or steel tension cable as you normally would.

Conventional fiberglass batting, as well as other materials, can be placed between the outer wall and the canvas liner. Possibilities include bundles of straw and sacks of diatomaceous earth. If you choose the latter, purchase diatomaceous earth in full granules—the type intended for swimming pools—not the powdery grade of material used for agricultural purposes.

COOLING

In the heat of summer, relief can be found by taking down the canvas wall from a yurt or by rolling up the sides on a tipi. If you're in a region with insects, hang mosquito netting on the khanas or

On this yurt, the clear plastic hub pops up to provide additional ventilation.

tipi poles. You may be able to control the bugs by rolling the sides back down at sunset.

In a very hot region, you can make your shelter cooler just by wetting down the roof of a yurt or the top half of a tipi. The evaporation of the water creates a cooling effect. For a yurt, you can make this a continuous process if you have access to running water. Take down the canvas walls and hang burlap around the lattice frame. Install a slow-drip irrigation hose along the top edge of the wall and allow water to run down the burlap wall, keeping it wet all day long.

A very attractive approach is to place trellises around your lodge. With climbing plants grow-ing on the trellises, you will have plenty of cool-ing shade.

VENTILATION

An important consideration in any season is proper venting. The natural flow of air through a tipi is usually adequate, but you may want to take some measures to improve ventilation in a yurt. One sim-ple way is to fashion small canvas "hatches" that are fastened to the roof canvas with hook and loop tape for easy opening and closing. These should be constructed so that they won't leak in the rain. To do this, make sure that the edges of the hatches overextend the holes, creating a shingle effect.

KITCHENS AND BATHROOMS

KITCHENS

Cooking can be done inside your shelter on a wood-burning or propane stove or outside in a solar oven. The small four-burner propane stoves that are made for apartments or recreational vehicles are very convenient, and some have an oven as well.

Cooking in a solar oven usually takes longer than by conventional methods. However, the satisfaction of using a renewable resource plus the slower pace of a lifestyle that includes time for this way of cooking are benefits not to be overlooked. You can purchase a kit to make your own solar oven or buy one already built.

It's important to contain food carefully to protect it from pests. Many foods can be stored in glass jars; just be sure that any jar you use has a tight, secure lid. If you have access to electricity, you can store perishable foods in a small refrigerator. For those seeking to live totally off the grid, there are plans available for building root cellars, evaporative refrigerators, and other means for storing food.

Equally important to food storage is the thorough disposal of any food remnants. Haphazard dumping of food scraps is certain to attract unwanted animals and other pests.

Washing dishes can be done wherever it's most convenient. If space is at a premium, you can set up a dish washing station outside, using a wash basin and water heated on the stove. An inside sink is handy, but you will have to carry the used water outside or set up a drainage system. Grey water can be used for plants as long as you use dish soap that won't harm the plants. A summer outdoor kitchen in the open air with a cool, shady roof trellis can be most enjoyable.

Numerous creative possibilities exist for counters and shelves. You can custom build whatever strikes your fancy, and mail-order companies carry storage units for any type of space.

BATHROOMS

Depending upon your taste and finances, bathrooms can run the gamut from primitive to state-of-the-art. The more permanent you make your shelter, the more important will be your choice of facilities. What may seem adventurous for a two-week vacation might become uncomfortable month after month.

Over the years I've experimented with many types of bathrooms for long-term use. One of the most satisfactory arrangements is to have a separate bathhouse building with a propane heater and a composting toilet. With a yurt, an effective way to accomplish this—and keep the bathroom nearby—is to have a smaller, satellite yurt off the larger shelter (Fig. 1). Simply install a second door in the main yurt and face the doors of the two yurts together so that you can walk right into the smaller one.

There's no requirement that your bathhouse must mimic the appearance of your shelter, however. It can be constructed fairly simply by using poles and canvas, or you can build a more elaborate structure of wood.

BATHING FACILITIES

To provide a comfortable bath or shower, you must satisfy three requirements: an adequate water supply, a source of heat, and good drainage. Sufficient water to fill a tub or create a shower can be obtained from a hose connected to a spigot, or it can be stored in some sort of container prior to your needing it. Water can be heated with propane, wood, or solar energy. When you are finished bathing, the water must have adequate means to drain away from your shelter.

During the summer in most climates, it's easy to set up a simple solar shower. The simplest method is to run a long black hose along the ground, where the sunlight will heat the water inside. This provides a toasty, albeit quick, shower on sunny days. For a somewhat longer-lasting shower, you can make or purchase a solar shower unit that consists of a thick black plastic bag and hose. Another option is to store water in a metal barrel, painted black for optimum energy absorption.

Above-ground tubs are an obvious choice for those who prefer baths to showers. For a long-term arrangement, it's even possible to build a bathtub that is sunken into the ground. Make the tub by digging a hole in the floor of your lodge and sealing the earth with cement, tile, or another material that will hold water. Providing adequate drainage is especially important for a below-ground tub to work, and this is easiest if your shelter is on a hillside.

TOILETS

Composting toilets work using the same process that converts your kitchen and yard waste into valuable soil conditioner. When built and functioning properly, they have practically no odor. They're best suited for warmer weather, however, since the composting action slows when the surrounding temperature falls below 55 to 60 degrees. It takes significant effort to build and maintain a composting toilet, but you can purchase complete, self-contained units that are easy to install.

The solar toilet is a wonderful approach when you have several people living on undeveloped land. It renders its contents into ash in a very short time. The high mineral content of the ash makes it useful in a garden, and it won't harm the plants. For this system to work, you must live in a region that receives at least 200 sunny days a year.

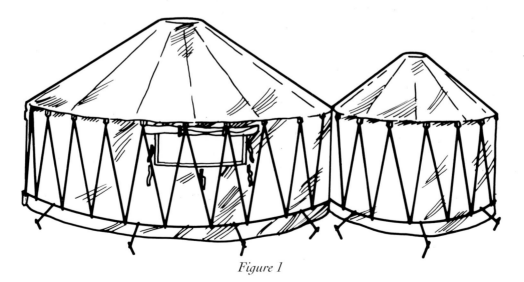

Figure 1

DECKS AND OTHER STRUCTURES

This raised deck makes an ideal space for outdoor activities or extra storage.

WOODEN DECK

With a relatively modest investment of time and money, you can build a simple wooden deck that will add substantially to the long-term enjoyment of your tipi or yurt. There are many plans and books available that describe how to build decks in various sizes and shapes. The simplest option is to build a square or rectangular deck, but your deck may be circular or some other shape instead.

If a less permanent structure is desired, you can make a modular wooden deck that is easily disassembled. This type of deck is constructed in sections that are held together with bolts. For a structure that can be taken apart completely, use screws rather than nails for constructing the individual sections.

When choosing or designing your own plan for a deck, consider the characteristics of your site.

Most plans are suitable for a flat site without obstructions. If you're building on a slope, you will need a plan that includes the appropriate bracing.

Availability is one factor, but your decision regarding what type of lumber to use will likely depend upon how much money you want to spend. Redwood, cedar, and pressure-treated wood are the longest lasting materials for decks, but they're also the most expensive. The sales people at your local lumber yard should have some good suggestions.

BRICK PATIO

A simple alternative to constructing a wooden deck is to make a patio surface of bricks and sand. It requires almost no tools, and the most difficult step is leveling the site.

After making the ground as flat as possible, arrange the bricks on the site. Using older sidewalks and patios as inspiration, you can create beautiful patterns with the bricks. Dump a load of sand on top and sweep it into the spaces between the bricks. Continue sweeping until all of the small spaces are filled with sand.

With rain and wear, the sand becomes a packed mass between the bricks and holds them in place. The surface is firm and can last for several years.

FRONT PORCH

To provide shelter from the elements, it's easy to add a covered entry to a yurt. (This idea isn't appropriate for a tipi because the door opening on a tipi is made of canvas and has no framing.) Attach the framework to the door frame and cover it with canvas.

MULTIPLE YURTS

Building a smaller, satellite yurt next to a larger one was mentioned earlier as a way of providing a bathroom, but this idea can be applied to any type of separate room you want. It's also possible to have one central yurt with many satellite yurts around it. Simply add another door in the main yurt to give access to each smaller yurt.

Another idea is to create a central courtyard by placing several yurts in a circle. With some minor decorative touches, this can make a beautiful environment.

COMPOUND TIPIS

Methods devised by various Indian tribes work equally well today to join multiple tipis into compound structures. One easy approach is to set up two or more tipis right next to one another so that the poles intersect where the tipis meet at the bottom. Place the canvas over the tipis as completely as possible, using some extra canvas over the area where they're joined. This area has a fairly low clearance and traditionally was used as a separate "room" for children to sleep.

Winter can make access to a second tipi less convenient than you might like.

An even larger lodge can be created by pitching two large tipis a distance of 20' to 30' apart and placing a ridge pole or strong rope between the two bundles of poles. Lay additional poles against the ridge line and cover the poles with large pieces of canvas. Open the canvas on each tipi so that it overlaps the canvas on both sides (Fig. 1).

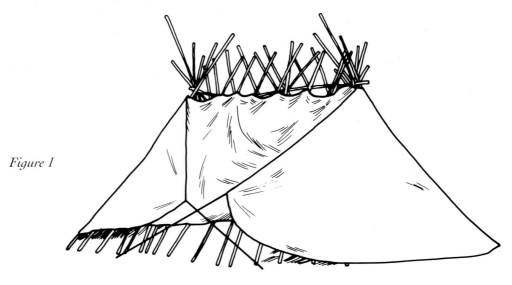

Figure 1

BIBLIOGRAPHY

THE TIPI

Baldwin, Gordon C. *How Indians Really Lived*. New York: Putnam, 1967.

Bancroft-Hunt, Norman. *The Indians of the Great Plains*. Norman, OK: University of Oklahoma Press, 1981.

Farb, Peter. *Man's Rise to Civilization*. New York: E.P. Dutton, 1968.

Jacobsen, Daniel. *Great Indian Tribes*. Maplewood, NJ: Hammond, 1970.

La Farge, Oliver. *A Pictorial History of the American Indian*. New York: Crown, 1956.

Laubins, Reginald and Gladys. *The Indian Tipi*. Norman, OK: University of Oklahoma Press, 1957.

Morey, Sylvester M. and Gilliam, Olivia L., eds. *Respect for Life*. New York: Myrin Institute, 1974.

Nabokov, Peter and Easton, Robert. *Native American Architecture*. New York: Oxford University Press, 1989.

Salomon, Julian. *The Book of Indian Crafts & Indian Lore*. New York: Gordon Press, 1977.

Wormington, H. M. *Ancient Man in North America*. Denver: Denver Museum of Natural History, 1957.

THE YURT

Brill, Marlene Targ. *Mongolia — Enchantment of the World*. Chicago: Children's Press, 1992.

Cable, Mildred. *The Gobi Desert*. New York: MacMillan, 1944.

Evers, Inge. *Feltmaking*. Asheville, NC: Lark Books, 1987.

Lamb, Harold. *Genghis Khan*. Garden City, NY: International Collectors Library, 1927.

——. *The March of the Barbarians*. New York: Literary Guild of America, 1940.

Onon, Urgunge. *My Childhood in Mongolia*. Oxford: Oxford University Press, 1972.

Phillips, E. D. *The Mongols*. New York: F. A. Praeger, 1969.

SOURCES

CANVAS

Living Shelter Crafts Tipis and Yurts, P.O. Box 4069, W. Sedona, AZ 86340. Telephone: (520) 204-1575.

SIMULATED SINEW

Crazy Crow, P.O. Box 314, Dennison, TX 75020. Telephone: (903) 463-1366.

TIPI POLES

Crazy Crow, P.O. Box 314, Dennison, TX 75020. Telephone: (903) 463-1366.

Grey Owl Indian Craft Company. P.O. Box 340468, Jamaica, NY 11434. Telephone: (718) 341-4000.

Living Shelter Crafts Tipis and Yurts, P.O. Box 4069, W. Sedona, AZ 86340. Telephone: (520) 204-1575.

Nomadics Tipimakers, 17671 Snow Creek Rd., Bend, OR 97701. Telephone: (503) 389-3980.

CLING-ONS

Living Shelter Crafts Tipis and Yurts, P.O. Box 4069, W. Sedona, AZ 86340. Telephone: (520) 204-1575.

Simpson Strong-Tie Co., 1450 Doolittle Dr., P.O. Box 1568, San Leandro, CA 94577. Telephone: (415) 562-7946.

YURTS

The Yurt Foundation, (wooden yurts) Bucks Harbor, Machiasport, ME 14655.

SOLAR PRODUCTS

Backwoods Solar Electric Systems, 8530 Rapid Lightning Creek Rd., Sandpoint, ID 83864. Telephone: (208) 263-4290.

McCracken Solar Co., 71 S. Warner St., Alturas, CA 96101-3672. Telephone: (916) 233-3175.

Real Goods, 966 Mazzoni St., Ukiah, CA 95482. Telephone: (707) 468-9214.

Soltek Solar Energy Ltd., #2-745 Vanalman, Victoria BC V8Z 3B6 Canada. Telephone: (604) 727-7720.

Sunlight Works, P.O. Box 3386, West Sedona, AZ 86340. Telephone: (602) 282-1344.

STRAW BALE

Black Range Films (straw bale workshop video), Star Route 2, Box 119, Kingston, NM 88042. Telephone: (505) 895-5652.

The Last Straw, Out on Bale (un)Ltd., 1037 East Linden St., Tucson, AZ 85719.

Straw Bale Construction Management, 31 Old Arroyo Chamiso, Santa Fe, NM 87505. Telephone: (505) 989-4400.

BATHROOM FACILITIES

Solar Survival Architecture (solar toilet), P.O. Box 1041, Taos, NM 87571. Telephone: (505) 751-0462.

Southwest Wetlands (constructive wetlands), 901 W. San Mateo, Suite M, Santa Fe, NM 87505. Telephone: (505) 988-7453.

Stewardship Community (solar mouldering toilet), John Cruickshank, c/o Sunrise Ranch, 5569 North County Rd., Loveland, CO 80538. Telephone: (303) 679-4274.

Sun-Mar Corp. (composting toilet), 5035 N. Service Rd., Unit C-9, Burlington, Ontario L7L 5V2 Canada. Telephone: (905) 332-1314.

WATER PUMPS

Kansas Wind Power, 13569 - 214th Rd., Dept. TY, Holton, KS 66436. Telephone: (913) 364-4407.

Rife Hydraulic Engine Manufacturing Co., P.O. Box 70, Wilkes-Barre, PA 18703. Telephone: 1-800-743-3726.

FURNISHINGS

Hold Everything: A Catalog for Organized Living, P.O. Box 7807, San Francisco, CA 94120-7807. Telephone: 1-800-421-2264.

METRIC CONVERSION TABLE

INCHES TO CENTIMETERS			
INCHES	CM	INCHES	CM
1/8	0.3	20	50.8
1/4	0.6	21	53.3
3/8	1.0	22	55.9
1/2	1.3	23	58.4
5/8	1.6	24	61.0
3/4	1.9	25	63.5
7/8	2.2	26	66.0
1	2.5	27	68.6
1-1/4	3.2	28	71.1
1-1/2	3.8	29	73.7
1-3/4	4.4	30	76.2
2	5.1	31	78.7
2-1/2	6.4	32	81.3
3	7.6	33	83.8
3-1/2	8.9	34	86.4
4	10.2	35	88.9
4-1/2	11.4	36	91.4
5	12.7	37	94.0
6	15.2	38	96.5
7	17.8	39	99.1
8	20.3	40	101.6
9	22.9	41	104.1
10	25.4	42	106.7
11	27.9	43	109.2
12	30.5	44	111.8
13	33.0	45	114.3
14	35.6	46	116.8
15	38.1	47	119.4
16	40.6	48	121.9
17	43.2	49	124.5
18	45.7	50	127.0
19	48.3		

MEASUREMENT UNITS

1 foot = 12 inches = 0.3048 meter

1 yard = 36 inches = 0.9144 meter

SUGGESTED READING

BOOKS

Burch, Monte. *Building Small Barns, Sheds & Shelters*. Pownal, VT: Garden Way, 1983.

Duncan, S. Blackwell. *The Home Insulation Bible*. Blue Ridge Summit, PA: Tab Books, 1982.

Hennessey, James and Papanek, Victor. *Nomadic Furniture 1 and 2*. New York: Pantheon Books, 1974.

Jones, Thomas H. *How to Build Greenhouses*. New York: Popular Science, 1978.

Kern, Ken. *The Owner-Built Home*. North Fork, CA: Owner-Builder.

McHenry, Paul G., Jr. *Adobe: Build It Yourself*. Tucson: University of Arizona Press, 1985.

McRaven, Charles. *Building with Stone*. Pownal, VT: Garden Way, 1989.

Newcombe, Duane. *The Owner-Built Adobe House*. New York: Scribner, 1980.

Pacific Domes. *Domebook II*. Bolinas, CA: Shelter Publications, 1971.

Sandia National Laboratory. *Stand-Alone Photovoltaic Systems, A Handbook of Recommended Design Practices*. Contact the Photovoltaic Design Assistance Center, Sandia National Laboratory, Dept. 6218, Albuquerque, NM 87185-0753.

Scott, Ray G. *How to Build Your Own Underground Home*. Blue Ridge Summit, PA: Tab Books, 1985.

Smead, David and Ishihara, Ruth. *Living on Twelve Volts with Ample Power*. Seattle: Rides, 1988.

————, *Wiring for Twelve Volts for Ample Power*. Seattle: Rides, 1990.

Strong, Steven J. and Scheller, William C. *The Solar Electric House*. Still River, MA: Sustainability, 1944.

Sunset. *How to Build Walks, Walls & Patios*. Menlo Park, CA: Lane, 1973.

Gregory Baum et al. *The Earth Shelter Handbook*. Milwaukee: Tech Data, 1980.

University of Minnesota. *Earth Shelter Housing Design*. New York: Van Nostrand Reinhold, 1979.

Wade, Herb. *Building Underground*. Emmaus, PA: Rodale, 1983.

Wells, Malcolm. *Underground Design*. Amherst, NH: Brick House, 1981.

Wright, David. *Natural Solar Architecture*. New York: Van Nostrand Reinhold, 1984.

MAGAZINES AND NEWSLETTERS

Building with Nature, P.O. Box 369, Gualala, CA 95445.

The Gentle Survivalist, P.O. Box 4004, St. George, UT 84770.

Home Power Magazine, P.O. Box 520, Ashland, OR 97520.

ACKNOWLEDGMENTS

Heartfelt thanks to all who helped make this book possible,
including tipi craft pioneers and friends: the Mugwort Family Band,
the Inspiration Sanctuary Community, Tarenta, Charlie Storm Owl,
and Oshala Hunter; yurt design contributors: Karesz Vasvary,
Terry Bodkin, Rita White Bud, T'om Seaman, Key Man Jim,
Randy Riis, Francis O'Hara, Driten, Marcy Marchello,
the participants in the Circle Living workshops, and the members
of the Aquarian Concepts Community; those who helped with
research: Randy Riis, Edwin Zumallen, the staff at the Heard
Museum Library, and the Sedona Public Library staff;
computer gurus: Carol Bunyard and Delphius; special friends:
Kathy Sundown, Bill, Elma, Desmond, Lexia, and Taiwaney
(the wolf); and those who helped produce the book: Ramus,
Santeen, the staff at Lark Books, Leslie Dierks, Celeanus,
the Sister Spirit Clan, and Horizon Vasvary.

INDEX